The power of currencies and currencies of power

Edited by Alan Wheatley

The power of currencies and currencies of power

Edited by Alan Wheatley

IISS The International Institute for Strategic Studies

The International Institute for Strategic Studies

Arundel House | 13–15 Arundel Street | Temple Place | London | WC2R 3DX | UK

First published November 2013 by **Routledge**
4 Park Square, Milton Park, Abingdon, Oxon, OX14 4RN

for **The International Institute for Strategic Studies**
Arundel House, 13–15 Arundel Street, Temple Place, London, WC2R 3DX, UK
www.iiss.org

Simultaneously published in the USA and Canada by **Routledge**
270 Madison Ave., New York, NY 10016

Routledge is an imprint of Taylor & Francis, an Informa Business

© 2013 The International Institute for Strategic Studies

DIRECTOR-GENERAL AND CHIEF EXECUTIVE Dr John Chipman
EDITOR Dr Nicholas Redman
ASSISTANT EDITOR Mona Moussavi
EDITORIAL Alexa van Sickle
COVER/PRODUCTION John Buck, Kelly Verity
COVER IMAGES iStockphoto

The **International Institute for Strategic Studies** is an independent centre for research, information and debate on the problems of conflict, however caused, that have, or potentially have, an important military content. The Council and Staff of the Institute are international and its membership is drawn from almost 100 countries. The Institute is independent and it alone decides what activities to conduct. It owes no allegiance to any government, any group of governments or any political or other organisation. The IISS stresses rigorous research with a forward-looking policy orientation and places particular emphasis on bringing new perspectives to the strategic debate.

The Institute's publications are designed to meet the needs of a wider audience than its own membership and are available on subscription, by mail order and in good bookshops. Further details at www.iiss.org.

Printed and bound in Great Britain by Bell & Bain Ltd, Thornliebank, Glasgow

British Library Cataloguing in Publication Data
A catalogue record for this book is available from the British Library

Library of Congress Cataloging in Publication Data

ADELPHI series
ISSN 1944-5571

ADELPHI 439
ISBN 978-1-138-02360-4

Contents

ACKNOWLEDGEMENTS

This *Adelphi* draws upon a number of papers that were commissioned for a seminar on 'Currencies of Power and the Power of Currencies: the Geopolitics of Currencies, Reserves and the Global Financial System', held at the IISS office in the Kingdom of Bahrain in October 2012, with the support of the Bahrain Economic Development Board.

A number of people gave generously of their time to discuss the issues running through the book and to suggest changes to the initial draft. They include David Dollar, Stewart Fleming, Martin Fletcher, Edward Hadas, Stephen King, Jane Macartney, George Magnus, James Malcolm, Arshad Mohammed, Andy Rothman and Rob Subbaraman. I would also like to thank Mike Peacock at Reuters for his support as well as Nick Redman, Alex Nicoll and Mona Moussavi at the IISS for their trust and patience. Any errors of fact or judgement are my own.

GLOSSARY

Balance of payments – A statistical statement that summarises, for a specified time period, the economic transactions between an economy and the rest of the world. Economic transactions include financial claims on, and liabilities owed to, the rest of the world, as well as the transfer of goods, services, income and other transfers (e.g. remittances and foreign aid).

Basis point – One-hundredth of one percentage point, commonly used to denote small changes in the valuation of financial instruments.

Capital account – One of two components that make up the balance of payments (the other is the current account), comprised of the net total value of financial claims on, and liabilities owed to, the rest of the world. These include net foreign direct investment, net portfolio investment, net short-term speculative flows and net central-bank transactions.

Capital-account liberalisation – The removal of regulatory barriers to international financial flows in order to achieve capital-account convertibility (the ability to freely convert local financial assets into foreign ones and vice versa).

Current account – One of two components that make up the balance of payments (the other is the capital account), derived by adding net exports, net income from abroad and net transfers.

Deflationary policy – Macroeconomic policies that seek to reduce the level of aggregate demand or to stem the rate of inflation in an economy. The latter can also be referred to as 'disinflationary policy'.

Expansionary monetary policy – Macroeconomic policies that increase the money supply in an economy in order to increase the rate of economic growth, and in some cases to increase the rate of inflation or reduce the rate of deflation/disinflation. This can also be referred to as 'loosening monetary policy'.

Hedging – The use of financial instruments to offset potential losses associated with adverse price movements in an existing asset.

Run on a currency – When investors sell a country's currency en masse after losing confidence in the country's economic prospects and/or over the government's ability to repay its debt.

Quantitative easing – An unusual monetary policy device by which a central bank purchases large quantities of government or other securities to increase the money supply and lower interest rates.

Swap arrangement – A large variety of derivative contracts in which various assets or their associated cash-flow streams are exchanged between counterparties.

INTRODUCTION

By Alan Wheatley

'In the literature on currency internationalization, geopolitics rarely enters. The eight-hundred pound gorilla is sitting there, but hardly anyone, it seems, wants to talk about it.'

Benjamin J. Cohen

Before US-led forces invaded Afghanistan in 2001, the CIA smoothed the path by buying the loyalty of warlords with suitcases and knapsacks full of crisp US$100 bills. Secret agents nonchalantly dispensed hundreds of thousands of dollars at a time. 'We paid them to overthrow the Taliban,' a US official said. And then the CIA continued to pay the Afghans to keep fighting.[1]

Money buys power and influence, especially for a country that issues a currency everybody covets. Today, the currency in greatest demand, by far, is the dollar. This book is about the power the dollar provides the United States and the geopolitical implications of other currencies challenging its dominance.

Alan Wheatley is Global Economics Correspondent at Reuters.

Currencies serve as a unit of account for denominating goods, services and financial securities; as a medium of exchange for settling transactions; and as a store of value for saving. Many currencies fulfil these functions only within national borders. But some are used internationally as a unit of account. The US dollar, for example, is the preferred currency in foreign trade. Central banks around the world also rely on widely used currencies, such as the dollar and euro, as a peg or as part of a basket of monies against which they manage their exchange rates.

Internationalised currencies are used as a medium of exchange by businesses to settle trade and financial deals. On a more informal basis, they are commonly accepted by shops and small traders in neighbouring countries, especially close to the border.

These functions may be a source of pride for the issuing country and of convenience for its citizens. But they confer little power – with one significant exception, described below.

Few internationalised currencies grow into reserve currencies, meaning they are kept in reserve by central banks (as well as by other official and private investment institutions) as a store of value. Central banks typically hold a selection of currencies in their reserves to match emergency import and debt-servicing needs. But one reserve currency towers above the rest, and that is the dollar. The US currency is frequently sought after for cross-border trade and securities business, and simply to keep on deposit. Demand for dollars is so great that it offers the United States an unrivalled range of overlapping financial and political powers to influence the behaviour of others – including the capacity to mobilise real resources in exchange for banknotes that cost almost nothing to print, as the CIA did in Afghanistan. The dollar derives further power from its use as a medium of exchange. Because the dollar is used ubiquitously, Washington is able to exert pressure on uncooperative governments by threatening to exclude them from the US banking system, thus blocking a critical channel for trade payments.

Chapter One of this book explores how the US has readily used the 'exorbitant privilege' conferred by the dollar to further its geo-economic goals. Among other benefits, the dollar's primacy enables the US government and households to accumulate debts on a scale that in other countries would risk a crisis of creditor confidence. By being allowed to live beyond its means, the US can therefore more readily afford the armed forces that underpin its global role. This clout in turn enables the US to shift the onus of adjusting macroeconomic imbalances on to others, especially allies such as Japan for whom allegiance to the dollar is a tacit quid pro quo for US military protection.

Chapter Two assesses the prospects of other currencies challenging the dollar's dominance: specifically, the euro and the renminbi. For either, significant challenges lie ahead if they seek to rival the dollar's supremacy.

The dollar's dominance of international finance confers a further power that is unique to the United States. Because all dollar payments are cleared through the Federal Reserve, the US can threaten to cut off any financial institution dealing with a country that is the target of international sanctions. For John Williamson in Chapter Three, this capacity to enforce a financial blockade, such as the one in place against Iran, is the principal way in which US power is enhanced by virtue of the dollar's widespread private use. In an age of instantaneous cross-border money transfers, financial sanctions are the modern-day version of gunboat diplomacy. Giri Rajendran in Chapter Four provides a comprehensive review of how the US has used the dollar-payments system as a choke point to bring Iran to heel.

These various forms of power and influence together have made the dollar a quasi-natural monopoly as the 'international cash'.[2] The dollar's popularity is self-reinforcing. Nervous investors instinctively seek the safe harbour of the dollar. Travellers unsure which currency to take overseas turn, by default, to the dollar. There are other feedback loops. Oil and other major commodities are priced in dollars, creating additional demand for the US currency and further entrenching its supremacy. As Williamson explains, the dollar is the most widely used currency not only in invoicing foreign trade but also in foreign-exchange trading and in denominating international bond transactions. More than half of cross-border loans and deposits are in dollars and central banks hold more than 60% of their reserves in dollars. This is because countries manage their exchange rates by pegging to the dollar, to varying degrees, more than to any other currency. This is critical to understanding why the dollar is the 'sun in the system'.[3] If a country's exchange-rate policy is based on tracking the dollar, it needs dollars in order to intervene in the currency markets and to smooth lumpy trade and financial flows. This strengthens the US currency's gravitational pull so much that even countries whose trade and financial dealings are not dominated by the US cannot ignore the dollar if they wish to keep their own currencies broadly stable.[4] For the US, these are the most virtuous of circles.

Changing times

It is impossible to know exactly when the dollar's attraction may fade and, with it, the geo-economic power it bestows. As early as the 1960s, the chairman of the Federal Reserve issued a warning that the dollar's stability would be more important, in the end, to waging and winning the Cold War than the precise number of US troops deployed in Germany.[5] What can be said is that the international monetary system is becoming more unstable, not less, as the global financial crisis that erupted in 2008 demonstrated. One illustration of macroeconomic and financial imbalances is the dramatic acceleration in the accumulation of reserves, especially by developing countries, since the turn of the millennium. Global reserves surged to US$11.14 trillion by mid-2013 from US$2tr in 2001, with emerging economies increasing their share from 38% to 66% over that period. China alone now has US$3.66tr in reserves, accumulated as insurance but generated initially as part of a deliberate policy to buy dollars to hold down the renminbi's exchange rate and so to boost export industries. Are there limits to how much safe debt the US can issue to meet the demand of surplus countries? In other words, how much more debt can the US accrue without undermining the solvency of the government and, thereby, the very confidence in the dollar that makes those securities so appealing in the first place? While chairman of the Joint Chiefs of Staff, Mike Mullen repeatedly said that US debt was the greatest threat to the country's national security. Abandoning its usual caution, the IMF said: 'Absent changes in reserve policies, extrapolations suggest demand for reserves would reach levels insupportable by reserve issuers in the medium-to-long term.'[6]

At the same time, the dollar enjoys the formidable power of incumbency. Given that the US currency is so widely used, considerable inertia exists in the international monetary system. Contributors to this book generally believe that the dollar will remain the dominant reserve currency for the foreseeable future. Still, sensing growing risks, reserve holders have been diversifying into currencies such as the Australian dollar and Canadian dollar. The share of minor monies in global reserves has tripled in six years. The likely continuation of this diversification trend is a theme of this volume. In Chapter Five,

Harsha Vardhana Singh spells out why, in an age of shifting trade patterns and global supply chains, the currencies of big regional trading nations are likely to become prominent at the regional and eventually international level. A kaleidoscope of international currencies could thus be in prospect. But, as Chapter Three argues, only two currencies have any chance of approaching the stature of the dollar.

The euro, the second reserve currency, will have an important role to play in a multipolar currency order if the euro area draws the right lessons from its almost fatal sovereign debt crisis. The other potential rival to the dollar is the renminbi, which China has begun to promote as an international currency. Because the euro is a currency without a state, the challenge that the renminbi could pose is much more significant from a geopolitical perspective. The sheer size of China's economy certainly helps the renminbi's internationalisation. Nevertheless, daunting obstacles must be overcome if the renminbi is to become more than a currency for trade invoicing and is to account for a sizeable share of central banks' reserves. To create deep, liquid and trusted government bond markets which would meet reserve managers' demands for safe assets in the way the US does today, the ruling Communist Party would have to liberalise China's financial markets and largely remove capital controls. In doing so, the Party would deprive itself of the economic tools on which it has relied to buttress its monopoly of political power.

Still, the consensus is that it is only a matter of time before the renminbi becomes an international currency, if not an important reserve currency. In Chapter Six, Di Dongsheng of Renmin University in Beijing outlines the importance of the renminbi for China's economic development to date and how internationalisation of the currency will be an integral part of the new leadership's economic reform agenda. The reforms, Di argues, will help to reinforce the Communist Party's credibility at home and open a new, more competitive chapter in relations with the US.

Yuriko Koike, a former Japanese defence minister, writes in Chapter Seven that China will encounter stiff opposition if it uses its currency to advance its political ambitions in Asia. China's neighbours are suspicious of the motives of an overbearing single-party state that often acts with divine right, by dint of the country's size and long history, to advance its objectives in all domains, from trade to territorial disputes.

All in all, Robert Zoellick concludes in Chapter Eight, the world is dealing with the 'unfinished business' of Bretton Woods, notably how to resolve the global trade imbalances that preoccupied the architects of the post-war currency order nearly 70 years ago. Zoellick expects a new, competitive, multi-reserve currency monetary system to emerge, but not through any 'grand treaty or global convocation'.

The renaissance of a great power is unavoidably a source of concern for the current hegemon. As China rises, increased friction with the United States seems preordained in many areas, from the military to the monetary. Yet in neither sphere of power is an abrupt change in the status quo probable. It is tempting to interpret President Barack Obama's retreat from Iraq and Afghanistan as a sign that the global dominance of the US has started to wane. If US power is indeed in decline, the rise of China as a military superpower remains some way off. It was not until September 2012, between the two US withdrawals, that China commissioned its first aircraft carrier, the 50,000-tonne *Liaoning,* after a long refit. The vessel, based on the hull of an uncompleted Soviet carrier, was not expected to be fully operational for at least several years. Even then, according to the International Institute for Strategic Studies, the *Liaoning's* battle group would be viable only in a low-intensity environment.[7] Similarly, the renminbi did not receive its commission as an international currency until 2009. This book explores how the renminbi is faring and whether it and other monies will come to challenge the dollar's status as the undisputed currency of power.

Notes

1 Bob Woodward, 'CIA Led Way With Cash Handouts', *Washington Post,* 18 November 2002; Matthew Rosenberg, 'With Bags of Cash, C.I.A. Seeks Influence in Afghanistan', *New York Times,* 28 April 2013.

2 IMF, 'Reserve Accumulation and International Monetary Stability', 13 April 2010, p. 8.

3 Paul Volcker and Toyoo Gyohten, *Changing Fortunes: The World's Money And The Threat to American Leadership* (New York: Random House, 1992), p. 62.

4 Barry Eichengreen, *Exorbitant Privilege: The Rise and Fall of the Dollar and the Future of the International Monetary System* (New York: Oxford University Press, 2011), p. 125.

5 Volcker and Gyohten, *Changing Fortunes,* p. 36.

6 IMF, 'Reserve Accumulation and International Monetary Stability', p. 5.

7 IISS, *The Military Balance 2013* (Abingdon: Routledge for the IISS, 2013), p. 252.

CHAPTER ONE

The origins and use of currency power

By Alan Wheatley

'Great powers have great currencies.'

Robert Mundell

The projection of military, economic and monetary power is a defining characteristic of leading states. Each facet of power reinforces the other. It is no coincidence that for the last 150 years the country with the dominant currency of the day has also boasted the biggest navy. At the height of its imperial power, Britain readily dispatched warships to collect debts and protect its commercial interests, a practice that lasted into the twentieth century.[1]

Those days are over, but military and currency power are still part of a hegemon's arsenal. Today, that country is the United States. By issuing dollars, the US has tangibly lower borrowing costs, which bolster its economy, already the world's largest, and make it easier to pay for the world's strongest armed forces. This combination of economic and military might in turn makes the dollar ever more irresistible to central

Alan Wheatley is Global Economics Correspondent at Reuters.

banks and investors worldwide seeking a safe haven for their money.

The capacity to mobilise resources, in an emergency, with a reserve currency depends ultimately on the creditworthiness of the issuing government. The dollar would not be widely accepted today if the US had not built up a solid credit record over more than two centuries, dating back to Alexander Hamilton's insistence that the young republic had to honour debts owed to private citizens of countries with which it was at war.

Britain's superior creditworthiness was a strategic weapon in the Peninsular War against France (1808–14). As Peter Garber of Deutsche Bank recounts, Wellington's army was able to secure its local needs by paying with Bank of England notes, which were readily accepted, or with army bills. By contrast, Napoleon's army had to pay in gold – or simply grab what it needed – because Spaniards distrusted French paper. Similarly, the unimpeachable creditworthiness of the Dutch was critical in their triumph over the Spanish in their war of independence: 'They could always use their credit to buy mercenary armies year after year that they threw against the Spanish, which had no credit. All it had was its access to gold in the new world.'[2]

Today, the powers conferred by the dollar on the US can be grouped under two main headings.[3] Firstly, the US has the power to delay or deflect adjustments in its balance of payments so it can enjoy both 'guns and butter' for an extended period, rather than having to make a difficult choice between lower defence spending and lower domestic consumption. Because demand for dollars is so strong, the US has been able to finance big deficits on its current account – the broadest measure of trade in goods and services and other current payments such as investment income. Any other country deep in debt might well have been forced, by financial-market pressure, to cut spending and raise taxes or even to turn to the IMF for a bailout. This was the fate of Greece and others on the periphery of the euro area. It was also a humiliation suffered in 1976 by Britain, having been supplanted by the US as the dominant reserve currency after the First World War. Yet the United States, by and large, has been able to maintain the world's largest defence budget while simultaneously running a large, consumption-fuelled shortfall on its current account. The US has had the related power to deflect the pressure of economic adjustment on to others, including its allies. Germany and Japan have in effect been blackmailed by the United States to do Washington's bidding, as explained later in this chapter.

Secondly, the dollar gives the US the power to persuade and coerce. No other country, for example, would have been able to use its currency to the same effect as the US did in Afghanistan. Could local tribesmen have been paid off in Swiss francs? They certainly would not have accepted the Chinese renminbi, which is not a convertible currency. But everyone takes dollars. While other states have accumulated large holdings of dollars that they too can mobilise, only one government controls the dollar-printing press.

And, if all else fails, the US has the power to coerce. Because the dollar is the ubiquitous transaction currency, and all dollar payments are ultimately routed through the Federal Reserve (Fed), the US can threaten to cut off any financial institution that deals with a regime subject to US-driven international sanctions.

Allies feel the brunt

What is striking in more recent history is the willingness of the US to deploy its own monetary power, and the influence it has over other currencies, against its friends as well as its enemies. In 1956 Britain and France invaded Egypt to regain control of the Suez Canal, an oil lifeline, that had been nationalised by President Gamal Abdel Nasser. The US applied fierce pressure on Britain, which was experiencing a run on sterling and the prospect of an embargo by Arab oil exporters, to pull out its forces. President Dwight D. Eisenhower blocked London's request for an emergency IMF loan and then delivered an ultimatum to Prime Minister Anthony Eden: Britain could either withdraw or face the financial consequences, including the US dumping part of its holdings of UK debt. With its foreign-exchange reserves running dangerously low, Britain fumed that it was being blackmailed. But the game was up. Facing a midnight deadline to cease fire, Eden capitulated at 5:00pm. The power of currency had prevailed.[4]

In 1944, the US had also flexed its financial muscle in negotiations at Bretton Woods over the design of the post-war global monetary order. It was agreed that exchange rates would be fixed to the dollar, which was convertible upon demand into gold. By the late 1960s, with the US balance-of-payments deficit widening and the Vietnam War fuelling inflation, the Bretton Woods system was on the verge of collapse. De Gaulle resented the 'exorbitant privilege' that the US derived from a system which imposed no discipline on its key currency. Only the US was able to pay for its deficits with its own paper money, making it easier for Washington to pursue its foreign-policy objectives and giving US companies the firepower to expand forcefully into Europe. A disgruntled France started cashing in its dollars for gold. Anxious that its gold reserves would be depleted, the US then applied 'extraordinary political pressure'[5] and extracted a written promise from Karl Blessing, the president of the Bundesbank, in March 1967 that the German central bank would not convert its dollars into gold on a large scale.[6] Dollar reserves had accumulated partly because of Cold War defence spending in Europe. West Germany feared that a run on the dollar would force the US to bring its troops home to shore up its balance of payments. For its part, the US administration was afraid that a withdrawal might encourage West Germany to develop nuclear weapons, inviting a hostile response from the Soviet Union. Currency politics and military strategy were intertwined: US monetary policy at the time revolved around questions of security in Europe.[7]

According to Paul Volcker, a senior US Treasury official before he became Federal Reserve chairman, Presidents Lyndon B. Johnson and Richard Nixon did not want to accept that their military options were limited by the weakness of the dollar:

> Consider the issue of maintaining our troops in Germany and Japan. It would be a gross oversimplification to boil all that down to a calculation of how many U.S. divisions abroad were worth how much loss of gold. But those of us on the financial side certainly thought that the stability and strength of our currency was important to sustaining the broad role of the United States in the world, and that consideration had to be cast into the balance of decision making. [8]

After the first oil-price shock in 1973, Washington made it clear to its allies, notably Germany and Japan, that the dollar would be allowed to depreciate unless they reflated their economies in response. As John Connally, Nixon's Treasury secretary, put it, 'The dollar is our currency but your problem.'[9] Motivated by security and economic self-interest in the face of a weakening dollar, they duly agreed at a summit in Bonn in 1978 to act as locomotives for the global economy by boosting demand. German Chancellor Helmut Schmidt came to bitterly regret bowing to US pressure as the second oil-price shock a few months later amplified the inflationary impact of Germany's expansionary policy. Schmidt failed to win re-election.[10]

The power to delay balance-of-payment adjustments, or to deflect them on to others, is another key attribute of a reserve currency. This policy autonomy was on display again in the accord signed at New York's Plaza Hotel in September 1985 and thereafter. Fearing that its record current-account deficit was fanning protectionist pressures in Congress, the US persuaded Germany, Japan, Britain and France to sell dollars in the foreign-exchange markets so that their currencies would appreciate. (The US also intervened heavily in the markets.) By helping to correct what was, by common consent, a gross overvaluation of the dollar, the Plaza Accord was a victory for international policy coordination. But the burden of the accompanying domestic economic-policy adjustments fell disproportionately on the United States' partners. As the US external deficit failed to shrink, Washington wielded the exchange-rate weapon once more: US Treasury Secretary James Baker threatened to keep talking down the dollar unless Germany and Japan stimulated demand to help boost US exports. The rift with Germany was so serious that it was a factor in the Black Monday stock market crash of 1987.[11] For its part, Japan had long subordinated its interests to those of the US, its former occupying power and now military protector. Fearful of offending Washington, Japan never diversified out of dollars. But even Tokyo was irked that the US was not keeping its Plaza promise and was not doing more to reduce its deficit. Toyoo Gyohten, a senior Japanese official who participated for decades in international monetary policymaking, recalls:

> On the American side, policymakers came to believe that the best and only way to deal with Japan was to apply pressure; they used the blackmail of dollar

depreciation and the threat of protectionism, while ignoring that part of the problem resided in the failure of the United States to do what it was supposed to do to correct its own fiscal excesses.[12]

All the time, the dollar was sinking. The Deutsche mark and the Japanese yen, on the other hand, doubled in value within two years. The Bank of Japan sought to cushion the deflationary blow by aggressively loosening monetary policy, helping to inflate a bubble in property and share prices that burst in the early 1990s thus ushering in two debilitating decades of low growth and deflation.

'A deficit without tears'

Japan's boom-and-bust was just one of many episodes of instability that have followed in quick succession since the collapse of the gold-backed Bretton Woods system in the early 1970s, including convulsions in Latin American sovereign debt in the early 1980s; the collapse of US savings-and-loan banks in the late 1980s; Asia's financial meltdown in 1997; Russia's default a year later; the crash in dotcom stocks in 2000; and, to top it off, the global financial crisis of 2007–08.

Yet, throughout the turbulence, the dollar's reserve status has been challenged but not overturned. Though the US currency's share of allocated global foreign-exchange reserve holdings had drifted down to 62% by mid-2013 from 70% at the turn of the millennium,[13] it remained well above the low of 45% reached in 1990 – around the time when the mark and the yen reached their zenith at 20% and 9% of global reserves respectively. If the dollar's role as a reserve asset is in long-term decline, the supporting evidence is not yet convincing.[14]

There has been the occasional year of crisis. In 1978, the dollar was so weak that the US had to issue bonds denominated in marks and yen, assuming currency risk for once rather than passing it on to others. The US did not resort to a standard IMF bailout but it did have to borrow about US$3 billion from the IMF in German marks and Japanese yen to support the dollar, which the IMF regarded as so enfeebled as to be unusable in its operations.[15] But, for the most part, the US has been able to attract private foreign money with little difficulty to fund its external-payments deficit. Because US creditors happily funnel their dollar export proceeds back into US investments, this has truly been a 'deficit without tears' as Jacques Rueff, Charles de Gaulle's economic adviser, lamented:

> The country with a key currency is thus in the deceptively euphoric position of never having to pay off its international debts. The money it pays to foreign creditors comes right back home, like a boomerang. The functioning of the international monetary system is thus reduced to a childish game in which, after each round, the winners return their marbles to the losers.[16]

The dollar's magnetic attraction

By definition, holders of a reserve currency may need to sell it quickly in the event of a crisis. US markets for bonds, shares and derivatives are unrivalled in their depth and liquidity. Central banks and big investment institutions know they can sell billions of dollars of US treasury bonds and bills without the prices flinching. Crucially, investors trust US dollar markets. Trust is a fundamental, if intangible, characteristic of a reserve currency, built up over decades as rules and institutions develop to ensure markets are not manipulated, contracts are enforced by impartial courts and ownership rights are respected.

Whether currency managers are right to invest so much trust in the US is a different matter. After all, the US devalued the dollar twice within 14 months in 1971 and 1973, and the threat of default can re-emerge if Congress baulks at authorising an increase in the amount of debt the government can issue. As the confrontation over the US debt ceiling dragged on in October 2013, China and Japan, the biggest holders of US Treasury debt, publicly voiced their concerns. Senior European policymakers warned that budget uncertainty risked endangering the dollar's reserve-currency status, as did credit-rating agencies, and President Obama acknowledged that the 'spectacle' had undermined the credibility of the United States.[17]

Furthermore, the US periodically freezes or expropriates the assets of unfriendly governments. The Treasury's Office of Foreign Assets Control was formally created in 1950 after China entered the Korean War; President Harry Truman declared a national emergency and blocked all Chinese and North Korean assets subject to US jurisdiction. More recently, Iran, Iraq and Panama have been targets of US economic coercion. As Peter Garber has remarked: 'It's a curious fact that the US since the Second World War has seized the reserve assets of many countries – consistently, constantly, regularly – yet there's an insatiable demand for US assets as a reserve currency.'[18]

The security connection

The trillions of dollars pouring into US treasury securities and other US assets are generated in large part by trade surpluses run by Asian countries and Gulf oil producers. These surpluses are structural – not a passing consequence of the business cycle – and have to be recycled in some way. Underpinning its financial attractions, the US offers the ultimate guarantee for risk-averse reserve managers: military protection. Cautious investors can rest assured that, unlike West Germany during the Cold War, the United States is unlikely ever to be invaded. It was no accident that before the fall of the Berlin Wall any hint of Soviet invasion or unrest in Eastern Europe would prompt traders to desert the German mark for the safe haven of the dollar. For their part, friendly governments may calculate that, in a crisis, they have a greater chance of being offered the shelter of US military protection if they hold a lot of its debt. This obliges some governments, especially those under the US military umbrella, to pay a 'security tax', buying US bonds with a lower yield than they could get elsewhere. In short, reserve holders are drawn to the dollar for reasons beyond the financial benefits.[19]

For the oil-producing countries of the Gulf, this security–currency nexus is particularly strong. All members of the Gulf Cooperation Council, with the exception of Kuwait since 2007, peg their currencies to the dollar. All host US bases. Saudi Arabia in particular enjoys a special relationship with the United States dating back to the Second World War. The US buys more oil from Saudi Arabia than from any other country except Canada.[20] In exchange, Riyadh spends billions of dollars a year on advanced US arms, giving Saudi officials privileged access to senior US policymakers.

Security considerations also drive reserve management in parts of Asia, where Japan, South Korea and Taiwan are under the US diplomatic and military wing. Even if there is no explicit quid pro quo, it is hard to conceive that they would jeopardise relations with the US by abandoning the dollar. Limited diversification into other currencies would be understandable, but a public threat by Japan in 1998 to sell US bonds, for example, as recalled by Yuriko Koike in this volume, has not been repeated.

Once again, the process is self-reinforcing. Because the dollar's global status adds to US hard and soft power, 'monetary autonomy … can make it easier to defend against political or military pressures from the outside.'[21] Thus, support for the dollar strengthens the US security umbrella which is one of the currency's attractions.

A qualification needs to be made, however. The US needs to keep a grip on its public finances to maintain the confidence of its creditors. The US administration is counting on a 'peace dividend' to cut the deficit following troop withdrawals from Iraq and Afghanistan. At the same time, it may be necessary to reverse cuts in the face of new threats. If the United States one day ceased to be the world's policeman, 'foreigners may no longer have quite the same desire for its debt'.[22]

Thus, military and economic leadership supplement each other. Adam Posen, director of the Peterson Institute for International Economics, agrees:

> It is not just that if the United States loses reserve currency dominance military activities will become more expensive to finance. If anything, major American military misadventures will also erode the willingness of other countries to rely on the dollar, and thus create a negative feedback loop between economic and security capacities.[23]

It speaks volumes, then, for the dollar's enduring appeal that the currency's global standing has not dimmed despite what many perceive as the twin misadventures of Iraq and Afghanistan.

The Asian model

The dollars piling up in Asia's reserves are the proceeds of trade surpluses that are hard-wired into the region's development model. In a trend begun by Japan, Asian nations have favoured investment over consumption and have cossetted export-orientated manufacturers. This requires central banks to keep their countries' currencies competitively cheap by intervening in the foreign-exchange market to buy dollars, which are then recycled mainly into US Treasury securities. China has adopted the same strategy and, although it owes no debt of allegiance to the US, has ploughed perhaps as much as two-thirds of its reserves into dollars. (Beijing does not disclose the composition of its reserves.) Since the Asian financial crisis in 1997, governments in the region have had a powerful additional motive to accumulate reserves. A sudden exodus of footloose global capital forced Thailand, Indonesia and South Korea to accept humiliating bailouts from the IMF. The ensuing economic recession and financial turmoil toppled Indonesian President Suharto and scarred a generation of policymakers across Asia, who vowed not to be put in the position of *demandeur* again. So they built up reserves as self-insurance – more than they could possibly ever need to meet import bills and debt repayments. This savings glut, as US Federal Reserve Chairman Ben Bernanke called it, was recycled mainly into dollars, pushing down the cost of borrowing in the US and thus contributing to the lending and investment excesses that culminated in the 2008 global financial meltdown.[24]

Soft power

Besides geopolitical clout, the dollar both reflects and magnifies US soft power. As such, it is an instrument in the arsenal of Washington's diplomatic power in much the same way that Apple products, Coca Cola, Hollywood film stars and the National Basketball Association project an attractive image of the country worldwide and so positively influence attitudes towards the US. A currency in broad circulation may become a status symbol – 'a visible sign of elevated rank in the commu-

nity of nations' – that shapes the preferences of others.[25] This
is significant because, in a fiat money system, where money
is not backed by gold or silver, a currency's value depends
on whether people *think* it is valuable.[26] Whereas governments may allocate their reserves according to economic and
foreign-policy considerations, others may take account of more
nebulous factors such as US cultural dominance.

This is not to say that soft power is so important that,
for example, the Indian rupee would replace the dollar if
Bollywood, India's hugely popular film industry based in
Mumbai, were ever to supersede Hollywood's appeal. Rather,
it is to argue that myriad non-economic influences reinforce
the dollar's hard power, and vice versa, making it the world's
'moneta franca' in the same way English is the lingua franca.
The greater the number of people who speak English, the
greater the incentive others have to learn the language rather
than another. The same principle applies to the US currency. If
most people use dollars, it is costly and inconvenient to buck
the trend. It can be done. Iran started to request payment for its
oil exports in currencies other than the dollar as international
financial sanctions bit. Iraq, before the US-led invasion, did the
same in protest against US foreign policy. But both these countries still priced their oil in dollars because that has been the
market norm since OPEC (the Organization of the Petroleum
Exporting Countries) switched to the US currency in 1975;
today the major crude oil futures contracts, vital for hedging,
are denominated in dollars. This is also the case for copper, iron
ore and any number of internationally traded commodities.
The ease of buying and selling dollars from banks anywhere in
the world also makes it the currency of choice in global trade.
For example, an exporter in Turkey or South Korea shipping
goods to Brazil or Nigeria is likely to bill in dollars and get paid
in dollars.

The benefits of the dollar's ubiquity

Feudal lords, or seigneurs, used to make money by minting coins. Hence the term seigniorage to denote the difference between the value of money – the interest earned by a central bank on the proceeds from issuing banknotes – and the cost of printing and distributing those notes. It is the equivalent of an interest-free loan. As Harvard professor Jeffrey Frankel puts it, 'just as American Express reaps profits whenever people hold its travelers' checks, which they are willing to do without receiving interest, so the United States profits whenever people in Argentina or Russia hold dollars that do not pay interest.'[27]

Iraq provides a vivid illustration of seigniorage. In 2003 invading US forces searching Saddam Hussein's palace discovered more than 100 aluminium boxes filled with US$700 million in cash, part of US$920m the dictator had looted from the central bank. The US$100 bills, some of them still shrink-wrapped, bore the print marks of the Federal Reserve Bank of San Francisco and other regional Fed banks.[28] Iraq did not acquire the notes by wiring Iraqi dinars to the Fed. It paid for them with the proceeds from Iraqi oil exports – real resources – that ultimately flowed into the US Treasury. As such, Iraq was indirectly paying part of the costs of its own invasion.[29]

Roughly 60% of all dollar bills circulate outside the US. The sum would be even higher in the absence of the 500 euro note, whose super-sized denomination makes it the bill of choice for drug traffickers, smugglers and other cash-only criminals in the euro area and its monetary sphere. (Saddam, incidentally, believed in reserve diversification. He also looted €90m from his central bank.) Nevertheless, seigniorage returns to the US are modest, especially when interest rates are low. Assuming an interest rate of 2%, the upper range has been estimated at US$20bn.[30]

In an age of global financial markets and electronic transfers, it is worth adopting a broader definition of seigniorage that captures all the economic benefits accruing to the US from foreigners' demand for dollar assets. Safe-haven demand for US debt has reduced interest rates on long-term government bonds by 50–80 basis points.[31] According to one estimate, the federal government and domestic borrowers annually save US$150bn.[32]

The US acts in effect as banker to the world, issuing short-term debt and recycling the proceeds through the financial system into overseas investments and equities for the long term. Because they are less liquid and more risky, these investments tend to yield much more than government debt. One study put the positive return differential for the US on its external balance between 1952 and 2009 at a handsome 2 percentage points per year in real terms and 3.47 percentage points per year since 1973. As such, by leveraging low-cost borrowing to buy risky assets, some see the US acting more like a global venture capitalist than a traditional bank.[33]

The euro area has also benefitted considerably from the euro's internationalisation. A flight to quality during the eurozone crisis drove down yields on German debt, saving the government in Berlin billions of euros.[34] And the euro area's gain on its net foreign assets has been estimated at 1.7–2.1% of GDP.[35]

The McKinsey Global Institute (MGI) argues that seigniorage benefits cannot be seen in isolation from the impact of demand for dollars on exporters and sectors that compete with importers. In a normal year MGI estimates the net gain to the US from seigniorage and lower borrowing costs to be US$40bn–70bn. But in a crisis year, such as the year to mid-2009 when safe-haven buying drove the dollar sharply higher, MGI estimates that reserve-currency status could have entailed a net cost of US$5bn. At most, the gain was US$25bn. It is not clear, therefore, that the US enjoys much of a privilege at all, let alone an exorbitant one.[36] John Williamson, in this volume, also judges that seigniorage is not substantial.

Non-traditional reserve currencies in 2012 made up 6% of total allocated reserves, up from 2% in 2006; and there is no reason why diversification will not continue. The prospects of some of these currencies are discussed in Chapters Three and Six.

The great financial crisis

The worries about international monetary instability behind the astonishing growth in demand for reserves reached a climax with the failure of the US investment bank Lehman Brothers in September 2008. The global financial system teetered on the brink. World trade contracted by a quarter as credit evaporated. The deepest recession since the Great Depression set in. What began as a meltdown in the market for sub-prime US mortgage securities mutated into a struggle for the euro's survival as several countries on the periphery of the currency bloc drowned in sovereign debt. This was, at heart, a crisis of confidence in the international monetary system – or non-system as some call it – that had evolved after the collapse of Bretton Woods. Here was a world of currencies backed not by gold but by faith in paper money and the governments that printed them; a world not of capital controls but of vast pools of cash crossing borders instantaneously; a world not of fixed-but-adjustable currency parities but of constant unpredictability in exchange rates. Central bank reserves have soared since the end of the Bretton Woods system: from just US$95bn in 1970 to US$11.4 trillion in mid-2013. The volume of global credit has also surged. In the US, credit-market debt outstanding reached US$41tr by 2012, up by a factor of nine from US$4.35tr in 1981.[37] In response, Asia, with China prominent, has chided the US for profligate fiscal policies and malign neglect of its currency. The price-adjusted value of the dollar, measured against the currencies of the United States' main trading partners, has fallen by more than 20% since the advent of floating exchange rates in 1973. It has also lost 80% of its purchasing power as measured against a basket of consumer goods.[38]

The criticism is only partly justified. The US has discharged the main obligations of the country issuing the apex reserve currency. Crucially, as discussed earlier, many economists believe it is insatiable demand for dollar reserves from countries such as China that drives their supply rather than deficit countries such as the United States foisting unwanted debt onto unwilling lenders.[39] Certainly, US fiscal policy has been lax, but consumer prices have largely been kept in check since Paul Volcker became chairman of the Fed in 1979. (A flood of cheap manufactures from China and other emerging economies has also helped to subdue inflation.) Moreover, the US has acted as a lender of last resort, providing liquidity to the rest of the world at times of crisis. In the dark days of September and October 2008, the Federal Reserve Bank of New York opened unlimited dollar credit lines through swap arrangements with the European Central Bank (ECB), the Bank of Japan, the Bank of England and the Swiss National Bank to keep banking markets liquid. At the end of 2008, these four banks alone owed the Fed more than US$470bn. In total the US central bank arranged swaps with 14 foreign counterparts and extended net credit of nearly US$600bn.[40] By comparison, the ECB opened just four swap lines, with Denmark, Hungary, Iceland and Poland, totalling €31.5bn.[41] This was a powerful reaffirmation of the dollar's dominance and the geo-economic reach of the US. Tellingly, when South Korea needed dollars in a hurry, it turned to the US, its protector, drawing on a US$30bn swap with the Fed, and not to China.

Yet power comes with a price. In times of crisis, the US in effect provides insurance to the rest of the world, so wealth flows abroad in what has been called an 'exorbitant duty'. According to one study, payments from the US to the rest of the world between 2007 and 2009 came to 19% of its GDP as the value of US overseas holdings fell by more than the value of foreign investments in the US. This is the flip side of the 'insurance premium' that the US collects in the form of high net investment returns in good years. It is a reminder that providing a global public good such as a reserve currency does not always yield an exorbitant privilege.[42]

The dollar's international status also forces the US to choose between higher unemployment or higher debt, according to Peking University professor Michael Pettis: when a country, such as China, builds up its national savings and buys dollars with them, it holds down the renminbi's exchange rate and drives US exporters out of business. 'The only way to prevent unemployment rising, it turns out, is for the United States to increase domestic demand in the nontradable sector by running up public or private debt ... So where is the privilege in all this?'[43]

The birth of a new order?

The 2008 financial crisis was not the first time that doubts had been raised about the sustainability of a unipolar, dollar-based monetary system. Indeed, in the late 1970s, after the twin oil-price shocks, policymakers beyond the US were so anxious about the glut of petrodollars that they seriously explored ways of reducing the dollar's pivotal role.[44] Over the years some wondered whether the US could continue to gain as much strategic advantage now that Europe had created the euro and Asia had amassed vast reserves, thus rendering them largely impregnable to US monetary coercion.[45] They questioned whether the US would still be able to exercise the dollar's power to deflect economic adjustment as it had done onto Germany and Japan in the past. The US could perhaps even be vulnerable itself to pressure from Europe's new monetary power. Would Washington still be able to attach conditions to IMF bailouts, blatantly furthering its national interests, as it had done to South Korea in 1997? (Seoul, with almost depleted reserves, was forced to accept an emergency IMF loan that required the country to scrap capital controls, liberalise its banking system and accept numerous demands that the US had been pressing in bilateral negotiations.)[46]

Although the dollar's global status has not suffered, the US has in fact lost some influence. Reckless US lending practices and regulation were the root causes of the global credit crisis in the eyes of many foreigners, who also blamed Federal Reserve Chairman Alan Greenspan for keeping monetary policy too loose for too long. Indeed, when Treasury Secretary Timothy Geithner urged EU finance ministers in 2011 to take more decisive action to tackle the eurozone banking and debt crisis, he got short shrift.[47] The US also failed to sway the G20 to adopt numerical benchmarks for reducing the imbalances that had destabilised the world economy.

Another sign of diminished US economic clout is that since the 1997 crisis no major Asian country has turned for help to the IMF, which is widely regarded in the region and beyond as being beholden to Washington. Of course, the fact that no big Asian economy has needed an IMF bailout is welcome. But the salient point is that the IMF is still held in such low esteem for its handling of that crisis that no Asian leader would contemplate stopping the accumulation of reserves and thus risk putting his or her country at the mercy of the IMF – and of its major shareholder, the US.

For its part, Washington remains publicly committed to a strong dollar – and the preservation of its role as the supreme currency issuer. And while the BRICs quartet – Brazil, Russia,

India and China – won slightly more voting power at the IMF in 2010, the US has retained its veto over major decisions.

The dollar remains dominant, at least judging by its share of international reserves. But the feeling persists that the current international monetary system is not working. The disintegration of the Bretton Woods regime had raised the question whether any one currency could keep the global financial order stable at a time of profound change, especially if that currency itself looked vulnerable. This question remains relevant today. The rough consensus is that the answer lies in the construction of a system where power and responsibility are shared among several currencies. What would be the catalyst for such a transition? The United States' allies in Asia and the Gulf hold dollar reserves partly as a quid pro quo for US political and military support. This is a bargain that looks solid for the foreseeable future.

Is US debt safe?

Arguably, what ultimately defines the dollar's dominant status is the US government's fiscal capacity to back the Federal Reserve's provision of dollar liquidity at times of crisis. This capacity is certain to decline as the global economy expands and demand for dollar assets increases; the United States will inevitably see its reserve-currency monopoly eroded. It could therefore only be a matter of time before the global monetary system becomes multipolar.[48]

Timescales matter. According to the ECB, the global economy is already close to operating with three regional exchange-rate anchors – the dollar, euro and renminbi – so the transition to a multipolar system could occur sooner than is sometimes asserted. Nevertheless, given the importance of financial deepening and integration in the internationalisation of currencies, any shift will still be gradual, the bank argues.[49]

This is also the predominant view among economists in China, including the head of research at the central bank, Jin Zhongxia:

> For the foreseeable future, we can speak of the global currency system as a framework of '1+4'. The dollar will continue to be the super reserve currency, supplemented by four smaller reserve currencies: the euro and the British pound in Europe, and the Japanese yen and the Chinese renminbi in Asia.[50]

The currency status quo is not easily changed, as the dollar's own protracted rise to the summit shows.

From the pound to the dollar

Because of the inertia built into existing arrangements, switching from the incumbent dominant currency is not undertaken lightly. So it was that the demise of sterling was gradual – more a dignified retreat than a rout.[51] The US had overtaken Britain to become the biggest economy in the world by 1872, but it took more than 40 years for the dollar to dethrone sterling. The First World War was the initial tipping point, as it exhausted Britain's economy and drained its treasury. Before the war, the dollar was not used as a reserve currency, but it quickly gained prominence and accounted for more than half of global reserves by 1925.[52] However, this trend was not sustained: sterling redeemed its position during the Great Depression as the US was unwilling to assume global economic leadership.[53] The Bretton Woods agreement of 1944 marked the second tipping point: it confirmed that the dollar would be the lynchpin of the new global monetary order. Even then, sterling was in great demand as a reserve currency for two reasons. Firstly, US balance-of-payments surpluses limited the supply of dollar assets and gold. Secondly, the 35 countries and British colonies that made up the sterling area pegged their currencies to the pound and held most of their reserves in London. It was not until ten years after the war ended, following a 30% devaluation of the pound, that the dollar's share of global reserves exceeded sterling's. By 1970, sterling's share was still 30% of global reserves. Even as some of Britain's former colonies grouped in the Commonwealth reduced their sterling balances, other countries in the Middle East and Asia were keen to add the pound to their reserves to reflect the currency composition of their debt and trade. Britain also rallied support from the US and other allies – manifested in a series of credit lines from major central banks – to manage the transition from sterling to the dollar, arguing that a collapse of the pound would destabilise the global monetary system at the height of the Cold War. The power of currencies was on display once more, albeit in a different way. As economic historian Catherine Schenk writes:

> More specifically, both Britain and the USA recognised that a run on sterling could only be stemmed by Britain's retreat from the international economy and an acceleration of the retreat of its global military presence. Thus, during the Vietnam War US support for sterling was often linked to British strategic commitments to Southeast Asia.[54]

Still, sterling's status as a leading reserve currency was doomed. Crumbling confidence in British economic management led central banks to diversify away from the pound, compounding the impact of OPEC's switch into dollars, and by 1976 Britain had to seek an IMF bailout.

The lesson to draw from sterling's demise is that deliberate management may be needed to forestall a precipitous rush out of the dollar, whenever its day of reckoning comes. Furthermore, although the dollar came to rival sterling in the early part of the twentieth century, the US had spent more than a century gradually building up its fiscal capability, its legal structures, its position as an open financial centre and a reputation for sound money.[55] That clearly has implications for China if it seeks to expand the renminbi's global role. Finally, public support played a role in the dollar's rise:[56] the Federal Reserve Act of 1913 paved the way for a deliberate strategy to carve out an international role for the dollar that would make life easier for US exporters and more lucrative for its banks.[57] The law was aimed principally at stabilising US financial markets, which had suffered another panic attack in 1907, rather than promoting the dollar overseas. But by authorising the new US central bank to discount trade bills, ending a ban on US banks branching abroad and creating a market in New York for trade acceptances, the legislation ended the quasi-monopoly on trade finance enjoyed by London, the home of the dominant international currency.

In sum, the dollar had all the attributes of a reserve money and was pushing hard to displace sterling, yet even then the two currencies coexisted for half a century. Will history repeat itself? Given the size of their economies, only the euro and the renminbi are viable candidates to rival the dollar. The euro is already a regional reserve currency, and China is actively internationalising the renminbi. The next chapter examines whether these two currencies are likely to fulfil their potential.

Notes

[1] At the behest of bondholders, Britain, acting with Germany, imposed a military blockade on Venezuela from December 1902 to February 1903. Britain was also part of a coalition of the willing that sailed in 1923 to protect debt collectors in Canton.

2   'The Geopolitical Impact of Internationalization of a Large Currency', presentation by Deutsche Bank global strategist Peter Garber at the University of California San Diego, 8 June 2012, available to watch at vimeo.com/44338726.

3   This categorisation is largely based on Benjamin J. Cohen, 'The Macrofoundations of Monetary Power', in David M. Andrews (ed.), *International Monetary Power* (Ithaca, NY: Cornell University Press, 2006), pp. 31–50.

4   David M. Andrews, 'Monetary Power and Monetary Statecraft', in David M. Andrews (ed.), *International Monetary Power*, p. 7; Barry Eichengreen, *Exorbitant Privilege: The Rise and Fall of the Dollar and the Future of the International Monetary System* (New York: Oxford University Press, 2011), pp. 154–59.

5   Francis Gavin, 'Ideas, Power, and the Politics of U.S. International Monetary Policy during the 1960s', in Jonathan Kirshner (ed.), *Monetary Orders: Ambiguous Economics, Ubiquitous Politics* (Ithaca, NY: Cornell University Press, 2003), p. 196.

6   See the Bundesbank's archives, available at http://www.bundesbank.de/Redaktion/EN/Standardartikel/Topics/2013_01_18_blessing_letter.html.

7   Gavin, 'Ideas, Power, and the Politics of U.S. International Monetary Policy during the 1960s', in Kirshner (ed.), *Monetary Orders*, p. 217.

8   Paul Volcker and Toyoo Gyohten, *Changing Fortunes: The World's Money and the Threat to American Leadership* (New York: Random House, 1992), p. 61.

9   Harold James, *International Monetary Cooperation since Bretton Woods* (Washington, DC: International Monetary Fund, 1996), p. 210, cited in Andrews (ed.), *International Monetary Power*.

10 *Ibid.*, p. 148.

11 *Ibid.*, p. 268.

12 *Ibid.*, p. 271.

13 Countries accounting for 45% of total global reserves of US$11.4tr in the second quarter of 2013 did not disclose the currency composition of their reserves to the IMF. They included China. See http://www.imf.org/external/np/sta/cofer/eng/.

14 Arthur Kroeber, 'China's Global Currency: Lever for Financial Reform', Brookings-Tsinghua Center for Public Policy, Monograph Series, no. 3, February 2013, p. 56.

15 United States General Accounting Office Report to Congressional Committees, 'International Monetary Fund Observations on the IMF's Financial Operations', Washington DC, September 1999, p. 34; C. Fred Bergsten, 'The International Monetary Fund and the National Interests of the United States', testimony before the Joint Economic Committee of the US Congress, Washington DC, 24 February 1998, http://www.iie.com/publications/testimony/testimony.cfm?ResearchID=307.

16 Jacques Rueff, *Le péché monétaire de l'occident* (Paris: Plon, 1971).

17 Paul Taylor, 'U.S. 'soft power' takes a hit over government shutdown', Reuters, 17 October 2013; 'Dollar's reserve role at risk from U.S. budget uncertainty - ECB's Nowotny', Reuters, 12 October 2013.

18 Garber, 'The Geopolitical Impact of Internationalization of a Large Currency'.

19 Eichengreen, *Exorbitant Privilege*, p. 134.

20 US Energy Information Administration, Saudi Arabia full report, 26 February 2013, http://www.eia.gov/countries/cab.cfm?fips=SA.

21 Benjamin J. Cohen, 'The Benefits and Costs of an International Currency: Getting the Calculus Right', *Open Economies Review*, vol. 23, no. 1, February 2012, p. 16.

22 Kenneth Rogoff, 'World is right to worry about US debt', *Financial Times*, 24 January 2013.

23 Adam S. Posen, 'Why the Euro will Not Rival the Dollar', *International Finance*, vol. 11, no. 1, Spring 2008, p. 96.

24 Bernanke was not alone in his analysis. Mervyn King, the governor of the Bank of England at the time, said massive inflows of capital to the West had encouraged risk-taking by banks on an 'extraordinary' scale. Speech by Mervyn King at the University of Exeter, 19 January 2010, http://www.bankofengland.co.uk/publications/Documents/speeches/2010/speech419.pdf.

25 Benjamin J. Cohen, 'The Yuan Tomorrow? Evaluating China's Currency Internationalization Strategy', 15 July 2011, p. 5, http://www.polsci.ucsb.edu/faculty/cohen/inpress/pdfs/NPE.pdf.

26 Kirshner, 'Explaining Choices about Money', in Kirshner (ed.), *Monetary Orders*, p. 262.

27 Jeffrey A. Frankel, 'Is The Dollar Losing its Role as a Reserve Currency and If So, What Does This Mean?', July 1995, p. 7, http://www.hks.harvard.edu/fs/jfrankel/DollarsDemise.pdf.

28 John Taylor, *Global Financial Warriors: The Untold Story of International Finance in the Post 9/11 World* (New York: W.W. Norton & Company, 2007), pp. 220–21.

29 Garber, 'The Geopolitical Impact of Internationalization of a Large Currency'.

30 Linda Goldberg, 'The International Role of the Dollar: Does It Matter if This Changes?', Federal Reserve Bank of New York Staff Report no. 522, October 2011, p. 7, http://www.newyorkfed.org/research/staff_reports/sr522.pdf.

31 McKinsey Global Institute has compiled a range of estimates from 30–200 basis points. See Richard Dobbs et al., 'An exorbitant privilege? Implications of reserve currencies for competitiveness', Discussion Paper, McKinsey Global Institute, December 2009, p. 42, http://www.mckinsey.com/insights/economic_studies/an_exorbitant_privilege.

32 Francis E. Warnock and Veronica Cacdac Warnock, 'International Capital Flows and U.S. Interest Rates', *Journal of International Money and Finance*, vol. 28, no. 6, October 2009, pp. 903–19, quoted in Cohen, 'The Benefits and Costs of an International Currency', p. 5.

33 Pierre-Olivier Gourinchas and Hélène Rey, 'From World Banker to World Venture Capitalist: U.S. External Adjustment and the Exorbitant Privilege', in Richard H. Clarida (ed.), *G7 Current Account Imbalances: Sustainability and Adjustment* (Chicago, IL: University

of Chicago Press, 2007), pp. 11–55; Maurizio Michael Habib, 'Excess Returns on Net Foreign Assets: The Exorbitant Privilege From a Global Perspective', European Central Bank, Working Paper Series, no. 1158, February 2010, http://www.ecb.europa.eu/pub/pdf/scpwps/ecbwp1158.pdf.

34 Jan Strupczewski, 'What taxpayer bailouts? Euro crisis saves Germany money', Reuters, 2 May 2013.

35 Christian Thimann, 'Global Roles of Currencies', European Central Bank, Working Paper Series, no. 1031, March 2009, p. 20, http://www.ecb.europa.eu/pub/pdf/scpwps/ecbwp1031.pdf.

36 Dobbs et al., 'An exorbitant privilege?', pp. 8–9.

37 Federal Reserve Statistical Release, 'Financial Accounts of the United States: Flow of Funds, Balance Sheets, and Integrated Macroeconomic Accounts', Board of Governors of the Federal Reserve System, Washington DC, 25 September 2013, http://www.federalreserve.gov/releases/z1/Current/z1r-1.pdf.

38 Sebastian Mallaby and Olin Wethington, 'The Future of the Yuan: China's Struggle to Internationalize Its Currency', Foreign Affairs, vol. 91, no. 1, January/February 2012.

39 Edwin M. Truman, 'John Williamson and the Evolution of the International Monetary System', Peterson Institute for International Economics, Working Paper Series 12-13, Washington DC, August 2012, pp. 16–19; Ignazio Angeloni et al., 'Global currencies for tomorrow: a European perspective', Bruegel, 23 July 2011, p. 35, http://www.bruegel.org/publications/publication-detail/publication/592-global-currencies-for-tomorrow-a-european-perspective.

40 Linda S. Goldberg, Craig Kennedy and Jason Miu, 'Central Bank Dollar Swap Lines and Overseas Dollar Funding Costs', Federal Reserve Bank of New York Staff Report, no. 429, January 2010, http://www.newyorkfed.org/research/staff_reports/sr429.pdf.

41 Joshua Aizenman, Yothin Jinjarak and Donghyun Park, 'International reserves and swap lines: substitutes or complements?', Vox, 3 April 2010, http://www.voxeu.org/article/international-reserves-and-swap-lines-substitutes-or-complements.

42 Pierre-Olivier Gourinchas, Hélène Rey and Nicolas Govillot, 'Exorbitant Privilege and Exorbitant Duty', Bank of Japan Institute for Monetary and Economic Studies, Discussion Paper Series E-20, August 2010, p. 1, http://www.imes.boj.or.jp/research/papers/english/10-E-20.pdf.

43 Michael Pettis, The Great Rebalancing (Princeton, NJ: Princeton University Press, 2013), p. 157.

44 Volcker and Gyohten, Changing Fortunes, pp. 152–60.

45 C. Randall Henning, 'The Exchange-Rate Weapon and Macroeconomic Conflict', in David M. Andrews (ed.), International Monetary Power, p. 136.

46 Jonathan Kirshner, 'Currency and Coercion in the Twenty-First Century', in David M. Andrews (ed.), International Monetary Power, p. 158.

47 John O'Donnell, 'Austria's Fekter says Geithner rejects transaction tax', Reuters, 16 September 2011.

48 Emmanuel Farhi, Pierre-Olivier Gourinchas and Hélène Rey, 'Reforming the International Monetary System', Centre for Economic Policy Research, 19 September 2011, p. 19, http://www.cepr.org/content/reforming-international-monetary-system-0.

49 'The International Role of the Euro', European Central Bank, July 2012, pp. 39–43, http://www.ecb.int/pub/pdf/other/euro-international-role201207en.pdf?2567d9aa903f78e891813ec6a8dbd27b.

50 Jin Zhongxia, 'The future of the international monetary framework', commentary for the Official Monetary and Financial Institutions Forum, 7 February 2013, http://www.omfif.org/intelligence/the-commentary/2013/february/the-future-of-the-international-monetary-framework/.

51 Catherine Schenk, 'The Retirement of Sterling as a Reserve Currency after 1945: Lessons for the US Dollar?', World Financial Review, May 2011, http://www.worldfinancialreview.com/?p=511.

52 Eichengreen, Exorbitant Privilege, p. 32.

53 Charles P. Kindleberger, The World in Depression, 1929–1939 (Berkeley, CA: University of California Press, 1973), p. 292; Jeffrey Frankel, 'Historical Precedents for Internationalization of the RMB', Council on Foreign Relations, New York, November 2011, p. 3.

54 Schenk, 'The Retirement of Sterling as a Reserve Currency after 1945'.

55 Alan M. Taylor, 'The Future of International Liquidity and the Role of China', Council on Foreign Relations, CGS/IIGG Working Paper, New York, November 2011, p. 7, http://www.cfr.org/china/future-international-liquidity-role-china/p26284.

56 Barry Eichengreen and Marc Flandreau, 'The Federal Reserve, the Bank of England and the rise of the dollar as an international currency, 1914–39', Bank for International Settlements, Working Paper Series, no. 328, November 2010, pp. 44–45, http://www.bis.org/publ/work328.pdf.

57 Kroeber, 'China's Global Currency: Lever for Financial Reform', p. 31.

CHAPTER TWO

The pretenders to the dollar's crown

By Alan Wheatley

'Some are born great, some achieve greatness, and
some have greatness thrust upon them.'

Shakespeare, *Twelfth Night*

The euro: a triumph of politics over economics

The single European currency is a political construct. It is
hard to argue that the diverse economies of the euro area
constitute an optimum currency area suited to a unified
exchange rate. Despite extensive warnings that they were over-
reaching, Europe's elites pressed ahead with monetary union,
determined to banish once and for all the spectre of war on
European soil. The euro was a vision cherished by a generation of leaders who had experienced the Second World War.
As German Chancellor Helmut Kohl repeatedly said, 'The euro
is a question of war and peace.' For Helmut Schmidt, the man
Kohl succeeded, the embryonic European Monetary System
(EMS), the precursor of the euro, was more than a currency
bloc too. It was fundamental to Germany's entire foreign-policy

Alan Wheatley is Global Economics Correspondent at Reuters.

strategy. At a historic meeting with the Bundesbank Council in 1978, Schmidt invoked Germany's shame over Auschwitz to overcome the central bank's doubts about the EMS. The Bundesbank feared that an obligation to carry out open-ended sales of marks to defend weak EMS currencies would undermine Germany's price stability and thus its money. Thanks to the Bundesbank's unwavering commitment to keep inflation low, the Deutsche mark had grown into a powerful currency, symbolising Germany's post-war renaissance.[1] So it was that Schmidt secretly agreed with Bundesbank President Otmar Emminger to exempt the bank *in extremis* from the requirement to defend EMS parities. In a display of brute currency power 14 years later, the Bundesbank used the Emminger letter to justify its refusal to intervene any further to support the Italian lira. The currency was devalued, triggering a run on sterling. Both Italy and Britain were forced to leave the EMS's currency grid, the former temporarily, the latter for good.[2]

A work in progress

A second geopolitical motive to establish the euro was to increase European standing in the world and diminish the exorbitant privilege of the United States that had rankled, especially with the French, over the years. In a 1990 report, the European Commission argued that the world economy would be better off with a 'more symmetrical' international monetary system – in other words, a world that relied less on the dollar and in which the US, directly or via the IMF, exerted less influence.[3] Protected by its single currency, Europe would be less exposed to the volatility of the dollar and no longer vulnerable to the US exchange-rate weapon.

With the launch of the euro in 1999, an assault on the dollar's hegemony seemed possible: overnight, a currency bloc had come into existence with a population greater than that of the

US and an economic output about three-quarters of the United States'. The euro's share of global reserves rose steadily to above 27% in 2009. By then, however, the global financial crisis was in full spate, mutating as it spread from the US to Europe, into a banking and government-debt crisis. Ireland, Portugal and Greece were forced to take rescue loans from a troika of international lenders – the European Commission, the IMF and the European Central Bank (ECB) – before the crisis spread to Spain and Italy. Interest rates on the two countries' bonds surged to unsustainable heights as investors questioned their capacity to implement the budget cuts and economic reforms required to meet the discipline imposed by membership of the euro. Because both countries were too big to rescue, the single currency's days looked numbered for a while. Existential concerns subsided only in the summer of 2012 when Angela Merkel, chancellor of the euro area's major power, came out in favour of continuing emergency loans to Greece. She supported ECB President Mario Draghi in his determination to 'do whatever it takes'[4] to keep the euro together, which he underpinned with a promise, if need be, to buy struggling eurozone governments' bonds.

Merkel, like her erstwhile mentor Kohl, had put the imperative of ever-closer European integration before the potential cost to her own electoral prospects of underwriting the euro. This was testimony to the geo-economic power inherent in a currency. If the eurozone had splintered, Germany would have endangered an overarching goal of its foreign policy: to be tied down for its own good as part of a European community.[5] The departure of Greece from the single currency area would possibly have opened the door to greater outside influence in the affairs of a NATO member strategically positioned on the alliance's southeast flank. Yuriko Koike describes in this volume how China has already shown keen interest in long-term investments in Greece. Cyprus, its banks weakened by their exposure to Greece, subsequently had to be bailed out too under onerous terms.

The euro's political lure

The euro's prospects of mounting a challenge to the dollar look bleak after these near-death experiences. But it would be premature to write off the single currency's chances. For a start, size matters when it comes to projecting currency power and the euro area, for all its problems, is more likely to expand than to shrink. Alexander Stubb, Finland's minister for European affairs and foreign trade, has said membership could reach 25 within a few years.[6] Two-thirds of eurozone exports and half of its imports are settled in euros. The single currency holds an especially strong attraction for countries that used to be in the Soviet sphere of influence. The Baltic states were the quickest to quit the rouble zone after the collapse of the Soviet Union in 1991 even though they had the most to lose because of extensive trade links. A very deep recession was a small price to pay for being rid of the 'occupation rouble'. The Estonian kroon was more than a piece of paper; for the country's first post-Soviet president, Lennart Meri, it was the flag of economic and political independence. The material incentives to retain the rouble were an irrelevance.[7]

Estonia eventually joined the euro in 2011. Neighbouring Latvia is due to become the 18th member of the bloc on 1 January 2014. Its government was so determined to join the euro that it rejected advice to devalue its currency in 2008 at the height of the financial crisis, engineering instead a 20% drop in output in order to regain competitiveness. As Prime Minister Valdis Dombrovskis said: 'Certainly this euro accession has a geo-political dimension to it. Just after we regained independence we clearly set our course towards accession to EU and NATO. We said to ourselves that we belong to the western world and that's where we should integrate.'[8]

The finance minister of another East European EU member state said he would feel uncomfortable staying out of the euro area for very long given the proximity of Russia to his country. Asked what security guarantees membership of the euro would give his country beyond those already afforded by EU and NATO membership, he explained that the euro was a 'lock-in mechanism, a kind of poison pill'.[9] Because the collapse of the euro would be a disaster for everyone, to achieve stability, the euro area had to be more deeply integrated economically. This required deeper political integration, and 'if you're not in that process, you're not really in Europe.'[10]

Smaller states typically seek shelter under the umbrella of a great monetary power. Several countries, including Montenegro and Kosovo, have unilaterally adopted the euro – just like Panama and Ecuador have dollarised. Bulgaria and Bosnia operate euro-based currency boards, while many other countries anchor their currencies to the euro in one form or another.[11] Most of them are in Eastern Europe but they also include the majority of France's former colonies in west and central Africa that were previously members of the franc zone. The experience of these countries shows once again that military and currency power are mutually reinforcing. Pegging to the French franc, and subsequently to the euro, was part of a package deal including aid and trade, financial and military support. The Africans could not pick and mix: 'Fear of losing privileged aid and security arrangements has raised the cost of exit for a number of governments that otherwise would have sought to establish their own currencies.'[12]

Unfinished business

Since the eurozone crisis began, the ECB, through its back-stop bond-buying programme, has emerged as a lender of last resort – albeit not fully fledged and only for countries using the euro. This also helps the euro's chances as a reserve currency. The ECB's pledge to do whatever is necessary to save the euro was matched by a recognition that the currency has no viable future without closer political integration. No currency union has survived in the long run in the absence of political union. When they agreed to create the euro after the fall of the Berlin Wall, Europe's leaders could not pass up a historic opportunity that had unexpectedly presented itself. Yet it was only 20 years later that governments began to determine the institutional underpinnings of the currency that should have existed at the outset.

How far the required integration will extend is uncertain. Some think that it is sufficient to pool bank supervisory powers, create a mechanism to wind down failing banks and harmonise national deposit-insurance schemes. Others argue that a much deeper banking union is required and must go hand in hand with more budgetary transfers to ailing member states in times of crisis (i.e. a fiscal union); and closer central oversight of each country's finances and economy, perhaps accompanied eventually by collectively guaranteed bond issues (i.e. a political union, favoured particularly by France).[13] The northern alliance of fiscally conservative states led by Germany is adamantly opposed to open-ended transfers but some politicians have not ruled out euro bonds as long as they mark the end of the integration process, not the beginning. If mutualisation of at least a part of member states' debt issuance were to happen, the euro area would be taking a big stride towards the sort of large, liquid, integrated bond market like the United States' that makes the dollar such an attractive key currency. As such, it would partly address the complaint that the euro is a currency without a state and so by definition lacks the independent fiscal capacity that is a fundamental characteristic of a reserve currency.[14]

The late Tomasso Padoa-Schioppa, a founding member of the ECB's board, insisted that the security of a sound currency cannot be provided exclusively by the central bank; it rests on elements that only the state or, more broadly, a polity can provide. To that end, the eurozone would need to take a number of determined policy actions to raise the euro's international status. Apart from issuing euro-wide bonds in order to remedy its inability to supply safe assets, the euro area must strengthen its internal governance, streamline its external representation, and extend the ECB's mandate and operational reach: 'At some point Europeans will have to decide if they want their currency to share the privileges of major international currencies, and if they are ready to equip themselves for the corresponding duties.'[15]

The chances are minute that members of the euro area will ever forge a unitary state like the US, thus curbing their ability and willingness to project military power – something that the political scientist Carla Norrlof argues is indispensable if the euro is to grow into a rival for the dollar.[16] But the EU already negotiates trade policy on behalf of member states and is making fumbling progress towards a common foreign and security policy. Some observers do not rule out a fledgling common defence policy one day: 'The day will undoubtedly come when Europeans, or at least a small group of them, will decide on a common budget together which will be devoted to certain aspects of the common defence policy. But we're not there yet.'[17]

The EU has shown a capacity to deploy money power of sorts by joining the United States in imposing financial sanctions against Iran. So even though the ECB has been strictly neutral on whether the euro should be an international currency,[18] it could still be used for geopolitical coercion. Such transitions take time. The US needed half a century or more to implement

Alexander Hamilton's blueprint for fiscal governance, so it is not surprising that the members of the euro area, steeped in differing traditions and protective of their sovereignty, are proceeding slowly.

The second tier

Reserve-currency managers are increasingly nervous about excessive reliance on the dollar. So while the US currency remains pre-eminent, the euro is holding its own and others are attracting attention. Confirmation of this trend came in June 2013 when the IMF started listing the Australian and Canadian dollars as separate reserve currencies rather than lumping them in the 'other' category. Glenn Stevens, the governor of the Reserve Bank of Australia, played down the shift as a mere 'classification change'. But David Marsh, a leading historian of the euro, called it an important step 'marking the onset of a multi-currency reserve system and a new era in world money'.[19] At the very least, the growing popularity of the two monies underscored some of the criteria that a country issuing a reserve currency must meet: a strong track record on inflation; liquid, easily accessible bond markets; and an impartial legal system that can be trusted to enforce contracts and protect property rights.

Sterling has also benefitted from diversification. Demand from emerging economies in particular boosted sterling's share of central bank reserves to 3.8% as of mid-2013 from 3% a decade earlier. But the increase is not by design: after the trauma of the protracted rundown of sterling balances, the UK does not covet major reserve-currency status. The same applies to Switzerland, but the Swiss franc, too, has attracted massive safe-haven flows.

The Japanese yen's share in global reserves is the same as that of sterling, having declined from a peak of 9% in 1991.

Japan had long resisted pressure from the US to internationalise the yen, only half-heartedly opening its domestic money and capital markets out of concern that demand for yen would force up the exchange rate and penalise Japanese exporters.[20] There is a parallel with Germany, whose central bank feared increased foreign ownership of its currency would weaken its control over the money supply and put upward pressure on the exchange rate, harming export industries. The mark eventually became an important reserve currency befitting Germany's economic might in spite of the Bundesbank, not thanks to it.[21]

As Japan came to recognise the growing instability of the global monetary system and the merits of Tokyo serving as a financial centre, it changed tack in the 1990s and sought to promote the yen and deepen its financial markets. By then it was too late. The economy was beginning a long slump that could be traced back to the naked display of currency power that the US had unveiled after the Plaza Accord in 1985. Tokyo's boldest attempt to seize the currency initiative followed the Asian financial crisis, when it floated the idea of an Asian Monetary Fund – under Japanese leadership, naturally – as a regional alternative to the IMF. The proposal was swiftly rejected by the US, Japan's military protector, and by China, its fast-rising rival in Asia. The episode was a stark reminder of the limits of Japan's monetary clout and a forerunner of political battles to come with China over Asian monetary cooperation.[22] As such, it served as an illustration of how the global order has an enduring impact on currency power and vice versa. The yen remains an international money insofar as almost 70% of trading in the currency takes place outside Japan. But with its population shrinking – and, some argue, for want of being an expeditionary military power – Japan looks destined to remain a subordinate reserve-currency issuer.

Trading places

Besides the emergence of the Australian and Canadian dollars, Harsha Vardhana Singh makes the case in Chapter Five that a number of other currencies stand to become prominent because of their significant share in regional commerce. Changing trade trends, marked by the proliferation of global supply chains, increasing foreign direct investment and the consumption habits of the swelling ranks of the middle class, suggest that some of these currencies will go on to hold sway regionally and even globally. As such, many more economies will have an influence on geo-economic relationships, he argues. Here, the BRIC economies loom large. Brazil and South Africa, the biggest economies in Latin America and Africa respectively, would fit the description of what Singh calls 'regionally internationalised currencies'.

John Williamson, in Chapter Three, believes India will be able to stake a claim to reserve-currency status based on its huge home market, a characteristic that he sees as decisive in setting the US and the euro area apart from the secondary reserve currencies. India has slowly started to show interest in promoting its currency. It gave central banks and sovereign wealth funds permission in 2012 to join the ranks of foreign buyers of government debt and in October 2013 made a big move to internationalise the rupee through a novel deal with the World Bank to sell US$1 billion worth of rupee bonds to offshore investors.[23] Although India's track record on inflation is unlikely to impress international investors seeking a store of value, the size of its population all but guarantees that it will become the world's third-largest economy, Williamson contends, thus elevating the rupee as a currency for trade settlement.

Russia's prospects of becoming a regional currency anchor are weaker than India's on some measures, starting with its relatively small and declining population. Furthermore, memories are fresh of Russia's debt default in 1998. However, within the Commonwealth of Independent States (CIS), Russia accounts for two-thirds of regional trade and its market remains the principal focus for many companies in CIS states, ranging from machinery manufacturers to service providers to agricultural enterprises. It is also the labour market of choice for Central Asians starved of opportunity at home. The establishment of the Customs Union uniting Russia, Belarus and Kazakhstan in 2012, which is expected to expand and become a fully fledged Eurasian Customs Union by 2015, might provide an institutional underpinning for the greater use of the rouble. Already it has boosted intra-bloc trade, and separate steps have been taken to use the rouble rather than the dollar to settle some transactions, including energy debts. In September 2013 Kazakhstan dropped its dollar peg in favour of a currency basket including the rouble.[24] For companies in the smaller CIS states that are focused on the Russian and Customs Union markets, listing in Moscow and issuing debt there could prove to be an attractive option. Because its putative partners (aside from Ukraine) are small, Russia has the potential to exert a powerful gravitational pull over a relatively small area.

As for the Middle East, Syed Abul Basher, a research economist with the Qatari central bank, argues that it is time for the members of the Gulf Cooperation Council (GCC) to abandon their peg to the dollar and establish their own currency. Despite high oil prices, the Federal Reserve kept interest rates low during most of the 2000s in order to stimulate the US economy. This policy mix was toxic for Gulf states, requiring them to import inflationary US monetary policy at a time of high and rising oil prices.

Furthermore, for the first time in history, the dollar persistently depreciated at a time when oil prices persistently increased. Basher draws the conclusion that the GCC countries must adopt a more flexible exchange-rate regime – and thus a more independent monetary policy – to deal with large swings in global prices of oil, food and other commodities. In short, it is time for them to drop the dollar peg of the past 30 years, especially as their economies are less dependent than before on the dollar and are more geared to the business cycle of Asia. Rather than just severing their link to the dollar, GCC states may go so far as to establish a common currency that could grow into a major international money in the long run. One way to achieve this is by pricing GCC exports (largely oil and natural gas) in the GCC's own currency. Pricing exports in the local currency will immediately create a sizeable international market for the new GCC currency. Given the imperfect substitutes for oil and natural gas in the world market, there would be a natural demand for the new GCC currency. A well-designed GCC monetary union could trigger a much-needed transformation of the economies of the Middle East and North Africa and may pave the way to an eventual pan-Arab monetary union, Basher believes.

That day, if it comes, is a long way off. As for the other putative challengers to the dollar, discussed earlier, it is hard to imagine them reaching a scale where they can be deployed for strategic political purposes in the foreseeable future. They might become currencies of prestige, perhaps of influence, but not of power.

China

The currency that has the best chance of growing into an instrument of power is the renminbi. Singh speaks of a 'sense of inevitability' about it becoming a reserve currency and says the disagreement is mainly over when it will happen: some see the renminbi widely used abroad by 2020; others think it will take a generation or more. The broad spectrum of views reflects a lack of clarity over Beijing's strategy. Indeed, does it have any master plan in mind for the currency? After all, China is in the early stages of deciding what sort of superpower it wants to be.

What is clear is that China has had strong motives since the 2008 crisis to reduce its dependency on the dollar. The near-collapse of the US financial system raised the spectre of massive losses for the Chinese state on its foreign-exchange reserves, which stood at US$1.9 trillion in September 2008, the month Lehman Brothers failed. In reality, the reserves were a sunk cost, an ineluctable consequence of China's development model based on holding down the renminbi's exchange rate to favour exporters. However, Internet critics wanted to know why China, still a poor country, was taking risks with the people's money, the renminbi, by lending the sole superpower some US$1,000 per Chinese man, woman and child so it could keep living beyond its means. The rumble of discontent was a reminder to the leadership of the Communist Party that holding massive reserves might provide insurance of sorts but was also a non-negligible domestic political liability were the dollar and US bonds to come crashing down. Of course, the risk of actually doing something about it, by letting the renminbi rise and scrapping capital controls, was even greater. Hence the policy choice to keep accumulating reserves, which had swollen to US$3.66tr by September 2013.

The global crisis also led to a sudden drying-up of dollar trade credit as banks around the world retrenched and quit non-core businesses. Global trade shrivelled, compounded by a slump in demand in the West as recession set in. In China more than 20 million migrant workers lost their jobs in a matter of weeks, many of them in export industries. It was a tribute to the capacity of the Communist Party to maintain social stability, and to the willingness of the migrants to 'eat bitterness', that they returned to their home villages with only the occasional protest over unpaid wages. But the mass lay-offs were another reminder to the Party of the fragile foundations of China's economic miracle.

Zhou's gambit

The initial response was the publication of a landmark policy paper by the governor of the People's Bank of China (PBOC), Zhou Xiaochuan, in March 2009, bemoaning the instability of the global monetary system and proposing a 'super sovereign reserve currency' to replace the dollar.[25] The political subtext was clear: the crisis had exposed China's strategic vulnerability. Here was the world's second-biggest economy – the inventor of paper money, no less – hostage to forces beyond its control. And all this despite its apparent riches. For beyond a certain point, reserves become a liability, not a strength. They are 'dead money' as far as China's development is concerned.[26] The reserves parked in dollars or euros or sterling yielding next to nothing could surely have generated higher returns if invested sensibly at home to meet some of China's glaring welfare needs.

Once recycled overseas, the reserves cannot be repatriated and spent domestically without the risk of causing inflation. Moreover, they cannot be liquidated without triggering the sort of panicked market sell-off against which they were meant to offer protection in the first place. A slump in the dollar would reduce US purchasing power, on which Chinese exports rely. As Williamson rightly says, one of the most concrete benefits to the US of the dollar's dominance is that China's room for policy manoeuvre is strictly limited. It is caught in a dollar trap of its own making.

For China, it is all the more galling to find itself bound to a country that it deems to be violating the implicit rules of the international monetary system.[27] In China's eyes – and many countries share its view – the guardian of the supreme reserve currency should not be running up huge budget deficits and habitually blowing easy-money bubbles that precipitated the dotcom share collapse of 2000 and then the sub-prime crash of 2008. As Zhou put it at the April 2013 meeting of the IMF, unconventional monetary policies were no solution to the problems of rich countries and could destabilise the global financial order.

Even as China launched an unprecedented 4tr yuan stimulus programme to cushion the recessionary impact of the global financial crisis, it decided it was time to shake up the system. Zhou's 2009 paper was more important as a declaration of geopolitical intent than as a viable plan to supplant the dollar. His idea of turning the Special Drawing Right (SDR), the IMF's unit of account, into a super-sovereign reserve currency never gained momentum even though it remains for some, including John Williamson, an elegant solution to the problem of excessive dependence on the dollar. But Beijing's initiative made clear its desire to shape a new monetary order.

The renminbi takes wing

How could Beijing hope to influence reform of the international monetary system as long as the renminbi itself was not widely used beyond the country's borders? Hence the launch, within months of Zhou's essay, of a pilot programme to pay for exports and imports in renminbi rather than dollars. Invoices would be settled in Hong Kong. The initiative made sense. It is natural for a fast-growing economy gradually to denominate trade in its own currency as market power allows it to deflect exchange-rate risk on to foreigners. Building up claims on the rest of the world in renminbi also means China is less exposed to the dollar and so has to worry less about capital losses.[28] Critics correctly point out, however, that China is tackling only a symptom of its economic imbalances – the currency risk attached to holding dollar reserves – without addressing the underlying causes that would render reserve accumulation unnecessary, namely an excess of national savings over investment coupled with a tightly controlled exchange rate and capital account. Moreover, the credit quality of the claims China is gathering in renminbi is assuredly lower than that of the US government, whatever its faults.

Still, taking payment in renminbi makes life easier for Chinese exporters and deflects currency risk on to foreign buyers. The accompanying birth of an offshore renminbi market, principally in Hong Kong, also gives China the chance to monitor the impact of banking and currency reforms in a semi-controlled environment. That is valuable experience for the day China opens up its domestic financial markets, which many say is Zhou's strategic aim in pushing the renminbi's internationalisation in the first place.[29]

The experiment has been a resounding success. Starting from scratch in 2009, China was settling 12% of its trade in its own currency by 2013. China is encouraging the use of the renminbi in overseas investment and is providing ever more official aid and loans in its own currency. The renminbi is circulating more widely in neighbouring countries, just as the dollar does in Latin America and the euro does in Eastern Europe and North Africa. In Mongolia, the renminbi accounts for 60% of the local cash in circulation. By October 2013 the PBOC had spun a web of nearly 2.2tr yuan in credit lines with more than 20 central banks around the world since 2009, including the ECB and the Bank of England. These are designed to keep renminbi-denominated trade running in case liquidity dries up and to lay the foundations for deeper monetary integration with the signatory countries.[30] In the same vein, at least ten central banks, including those of South Africa, Australia, Nigeria and Malaysia, have invested part of their reserves in renminbi bonds. Offshore renminbi markets have sprung up in London, Singapore and Taiwan, with others likely to follow. As Eswar Prasad and Lei Ye put it:

> These shifts, which are more symbolic than substan-
> tive at present, will develop critical mass over time
> and have the potential to start transforming the global
> monetary system. The Chinese government's recent
> policy actions are indicative of its serious intent to
> broaden the global role of its currency.[31]

In particular, the rapid expansion of different elements of the offshore renminbi market is an encouraging sign of the currency's prospects of getting a significant foothold in the Asian region's trade and financial transactions.[32]

As of August 2013, the renminbi ranked eighth in the list of most-used currencies for international transactions with a 1.49% share. That was up from a 0.92% share in January 2012, when it was in 13th place. In the interim, trading value in the renminbi had more than doubled and it had overtaken the Swedish crown, South Korean won and Russian rouble.[33] There is every reason to suppose this share will swell as the use of the renminbi in settling exports and imports expands in tandem with the Chinese economy. The bank HSBC expects the renminbi to be used in 30% of China's total trade by 2015 and in half of its trade with emerging markets. But settling trade in renminbi is an easy first step. It requires no fundamen-tal change to domestic policy or steps to remedy the weakness of the financial system, which many see as a major impediment to a greater international role for renminbi.[34]

The Party's dilemma

To take the renminbi to the next stage will entail nothing short of a policy upheaval. China's economic success has been built on the repression of market forces in areas where it counts. Unfettered competition reigns in many sectors of the economy, for example retail. But interest rates and the exchange rate are controlled by the Communist Party. Party-run banks are protected by capital controls from the consequences of any bad Party-directed lending to local governments and Party-run companies that dominate strategic industries. This will all have to change if China wants the renminbi to blossom into a true reserve currency. Foreign central banks and institutional investors will not accumulate the renminbi in any volume as a store of value – as distinct from a transaction currency – unless they can move their money in and out of China as they please. That implies flexible exchange, and interest, rates and banks that are strong enough to ride the waves of market-driven capital flows. International investors will also require a liquid, transparent market for high-quality government renminbi securities. China's bond market, though, is much less developed than most of its emerging market peers' and most paper is held to maturity.

Carrying out all these fundamental reforms would take years even if there was full political backing for them. But there is not. Apart from the central bank, which is a fairly weak institution in China, it is difficult to identify the interest groups that would reap huge benefits from ending the status quo.[35] The party-state proclaimed the objective of capital-account convertibility as far back as 1993, but controls on money flows not related to trade and investment are still largely binding. What's more, the 1997 and 2008 crises have been a salutary reminder of the need for emerging economies to tread carefully in opening up to global capital flows. China has allowed the renminbi to rise 35% against the dollar since 2005, but it continues to add to its stockpile of reserves in order to hold the exchange rate down. And interest rates are still tightly managed. These are the levers of economic power and the party-state is not going to surrender them without careful thought, for to do so could unleash economic, political and social forces beyond its control.[36]

The Party is in a bind because economic forces might overwhelm China's investment-heavy development model before long in any case. Central bank chief Zhou is pushing to free up the economy and markets because he knows reform is imperative. The economy needs market-driven allocation of capital, competition in protected sectors and rebalancing towards consumption and services.

Internationalisation of the renminbi would increase the competitiveness of Chinese financial firms by giving them access to a deep pool of offshore assets. A thriving financial sector in turn would help to achieve the goal of establishing Shanghai as a global financial centre. However, there is scant evidence that the Party is willing to venture down the path of radical financial change unless economic growth slows so sharply, or discontent over issues such as inequality, corruption and pollution multiplies so quickly, that it is left with no alternative:

> Judging from the carefully calibrated choreography that has been followed until now, it seems clear that policy makers understand that, eventually, diminished command is the price they will have to pay for an internationalized yuan. But in the spirit of Saint Augustine – who prayed to the Almighty for celibacy, just 'not yet' – it seems that Beijing would prefer to postpone the moment for as long as possible.[37]

Reserve-currency status would be nice to have. It would confer prestige and power – surely the birthright of a country with 5,000 years of history regaining its rightful place as the world's biggest economy, as China was until around 1820. The *Liaoning* is also an instrument of power. The difference is that building an aircraft carrier does not require the Party to run the risk of emasculating itself. Far from it: like China's space programme, the carrier is a source of pride and bolsters the Party's standing with the people. Seen through this prism, China may well acquire other great-power policy instruments before the renminbi matures into a major international currency carrying political clout.

But suppose this speculation is wrong and the Party strides off down the path of reform. The abolition in July 2013 of the floor on bank lending rates sent an important signal of an intent to liberalise, and speculation intensified as the year wore on that a plan for dismantling capital controls was in the works. The establishment in September 2013 of a free-trade zone in Shanghai with relaxed financial and investment rules was another harbinger of change. HSBC expects full convertibility of the renminbi in five years. The Brussels think tank Bruegel posits that, given the dynamics of currency reforms under way, over a 15-year period the renminbi can be a floating currency underpinned by fairly complete capital mobility.[38]

However, reaching the point at which the renminbi is on an equal footing with the dollar would require not only a clean break with financial controls. China would still have a lot of ground to make up to build the trust that is the foundation of currency power – trust in a country's markets, its institutions and its intentions. There are several points to consider. Firstly, in Africa, Chinese trade, investment and aid have given a remarkable boost to the continent's economic growth. But China has also generated resentment with its heavy-handed,

Sino-centric ways of doing business, prompting grumbles about a new colonialism.

Secondly, in Latin America, industrialists in Brazil and Argentina have bridled at the flood of keenly priced Chinese imports decimating local industries such as footwear. Brazil, alarmed by Chinese interest in buying soybean farms, banned foreign investors from purchasing large tracts of land.

Thirdly, in Asia, China has alienated many of its neighbours with its confrontational, nationalist stance on disputed islands and shoals in the South and East China seas. The issuance of passports with maps incorporating China's territorial claims sparked protests by a handful of states. China's construction of several dams on the Mekong has irritated countries down-stream fearful of a disruption to water supplies. China has also provoked India with troop incursions over their disputed common border.

Set against this, the country has no record of imperial adven-tures and insists that it is intent on a peaceful rise. Nevertheless, China's military build-up and its territorial disputes weigh in the balance when it is trying to coax countries to conduct trade and finance in the renminbi, according to scholars Xiaoli Chen and Yin-Wong Cheung:

> The persuasion goes beyond economic reasoning. Political considerations, especially in East Asia, could play a non-negligible role in choosing an interna-tional currency. The legacies of war, occupation, and communism have induced the antagonism towards regional hegemony.[39]

China, of course, is aware of the mistrust factor. An important reason why Beijing disregarded the strong advice it received from the IMF and others to devalue the renminbi during the

1997–98 financial crisis was to build confidence in the currency and establish a reputation for promoting stability at times of turmoil.[40] China's image had been tarnished by the Tiananmen Square massacre in 1989. With Hong Kong newly returned to the national fold, there was a chance for Beijing to gain credit by ensuring – as it had promised – that the prosperity of the former British colony would not be endangered by currency speculation. This required avoiding a devaluation of the renminbi.

Nevertheless, China is likely to encounter problems, and this is an argument advanced cogently by the political scientist Edward Luttwak. He chides Beijing for displaying 'super-power autism' and says the logic of strategy dictates that its simultaneous aggrandisement on the economic, political and military fronts will inevitably be resisted by geo-economic means because it ultimately threatens the very independence of its neighbours. An 'authoritarian, increasingly assertive China empowered by very rapid economic growth' is also prompting a number of Asian states to forge new military and diplomatic relationships in 'a coalescence of the threatened' to counter Beijing's thrust. Luttwak, who diagnoses China as suffering from 'Acquired Strategy Deficiency Syndrome', draws a parallel with the alliance that Britain and France forged to resist post-1890 German expansionism:

> As the strength of a rising Great Power continues to increase, friendly neighbors (sic) become watchful, allies edge toward neutrality, former neutrals become adversaries, and committed adversaries old and new are compelled to overcome their differences to combine against the Great Power rising too quickly. [41]

It is perfectly obvious in retrospect that Germany's strategy, like China's today, was doomed to fail; only a militarily non-threatening and diplomatically conciliatory stance could have served Germany well, accelerating its peaceful rise to new heights of cultural prosperity. One consolation for an excessively successful China is that Luttwak sees no 1914 end to the story in armed conflict, destruction and defeat as there was for an excessively successful Germany. The presence of nuclear weapons makes that impossible: 'Instead of a slide toward war, there is only the self-defeating process whereby China is uniting powers large and small against it, explicitly to contain its future strength.'[42]

Luttwak is confident that China will not ultimately 'disrupt the equilibrium of world politics' because the Chinese themselves will moderate their behaviour as they advance economically and culturally. In the interim, though, a geo-economic struggle is inevitable, involving barriers to trade and investment, more extensive prohibition of technology transfer and even restrictions on raw material exports to China:

> One force offsetting anti-Chinese sentiment is the country's thickening web of free-trade agreements in Asia and the influence of informal ethnic Chinese networks. According to one line of thinking, these will reinforce each other to consolidate the RMB's position as a credible regional currency.[43]

Seen in that light, it can be argued that transforming the renminbi into an international currency is meant to promote China's political and economic interests in Southeast Asia, which China regards as its rightful sphere of influence. That in turn could lead to the creation of a de facto renminbi bloc uniting the ten members of the Association of Southeast Asian Nations (ASEAN) with China, Hong Kong and Taiwan – something that Japan and South Korea, given their own economic interest in ASEAN, would find 'divisive'.[44] Antagonism on the part of two US allies towards China's putative ambition to lead an Asian monetary area would doubtless rankle with the leadership in Beijing, which already perceives that the US strategic pivot to Asia is designed to hold China down. The decision to exclude China from US-led trans-Pacific trade talks seems telling. So too does US President Barack Obama's choice of Myanmar, a semi-satellite of China, for his first overseas visit following his re-election.

A question of trust

China is paying the price for the marked lack of transparency of what remains a deeply Leninist ruling party. This opacity breeds suspicion of China's motives, as the country's natural-resource and telecommunications-equipment companies have repeatedly discovered in doing business abroad. The acquisition of land in Iceland by a rich Chinese businessman, ostensibly to build a luxury hotel and golf course, invited speculation that he was a front for nefarious state schemes.[45]

A great currency is built on trust in the issuing state – its creditworthiness, in a word. And China is discovering that trust and credit cannot be boiled down to GDP. When it comes to establishing the credentials of the renminbi as an international store of value, the fact that China is under the control of a Communist Party that brooks no opposition is likely to limit the prospects for the currency to play a role commensurate with the importance of China's economy.[46] More specifically, some go so far as to ask whether an authoritarian China could ever gain the market trust required to be a reserve nation.[47]

As Barry Eichengreen argues, China lacks the contested elections and political systems that have limited the arbitrary exercise of executive power in the US and Britain. Democracy matters for international currency status because it is elected governments that are best able to make the credible commitments needed to develop deep and liquid financial markets and to respect creditor rights. As Eichengreen concludes:

> This does not imply that China must have a Democratic Spring before the renminbi becomes a leading international and reserve currency. But it does suggest that it will have to strengthen the powers of the National People's Congress further and create a more transparent rules-based bureaucracy in order to achieve its monetary goals.[48]

Yi Gang, a deputy governor of the PBOC, counters that the political stability and predictability that the Communist Party brings are positive for confidence in the currency. But a country also needs military might and 'its culture's ability to attract people and money', Yi acknowledges.[49]

This touches on the broader questions of China's soft power. Mistrust in Beijing has hindered China in its repeated efforts 'to project to the world national values, ideals and quality of life that others can identify with and aspire to emulate' according to one European commentator.[50] This reasoning is provocative to Beijing. A prominent Chinese academic, Yao Yang, maintains that if the West demands a complete social and political transformation in China before treating it as an equal, that will be a 'major source of tension' in years to come.[51] But *Caixin*, a respected Chinese newsweekly, concedes that China needs to increase its 'moral appeal' to neighbouring countries and 'do much more to dispel their doubts and worries'.[52]

Potentially, the renminbi could be central to Chinese soft power and President Xi Jinping's ill-defined notion of a 'Chinese Dream'. For as the Austrian economist Joseph Schumpeter put it, the culture of a nation and its currency are two sides of the same coin:

> The often passionate, always great interest that is paid to the practical questions of the monetary system and the value of money can only be explained by the fact that the monetary system of a people reflects all that that people wants, does, endures, is. [53]

Notes

[1] By the late 1980s, the mark accounted for 20% of global central bank reserves; more than 80% of German exports and 50% of imports were denominated in marks. Arthur Kroeber, 'RMB Rising: Lessons from History', *China Economic Quarterly*, March 2012, pp. 35–36.

[2] David Marsh, *The Euro: The Battle for the New Global Currency* (New Haven, CT: Yale University Press, 2011), pp. 166–69.

[3] Commission of the European Communities, 'One market, one money: An evaluation of the potential benefits and costs of forming an economic and monetary union', *European Economy*, no. 44, October 1990.

[4] Comments by ECB President Mario Draghi in London, 26 July 2012, http://www.ecb.int/press/key/date/2012/html/sp120726.en.html.

[5] Jeffrey Frankel, 'Historical Precedents for Internationalization of the RMB', Council on Foreign Relations, New York, November 2011, p. 7.

[6] Kati Pohjanpalo, 'Euro Can Grow to 25 States in Next Years in Finnish Scenario', Bloomberg, 6 May 2013.

[7] Rawi Abdelal, 'National Strategy and National Money, Politics and the End of the Ruble Zone 1991–94', in Jonathan Kirshner (ed.), *Monetary Orders: Ambiguous Economics, Ubiquitous Politics* (Ithaca, NY: Cornell University Press, 2003), p. 101.

[8] Interview with the author in Riga, March 2013.

[9] Interview with the author in London, February 2013.

[10] *Ibid.*

[11] 'The International Role of the Euro', European Central Bank, July 2013, p. 68, http://www.ecb.europa.eu/pub/pdf/other/euro-international-role201307en.pdf. Countries using the euro as a reference currency include Switzerland, which in September 2011 unilaterally announced a minimum exchange rate of 1.20 Swiss francs per euro.

[12] David Stasavage, 'When Do States Abandon Monetary Discretion? Lessons from the Evolution of the

CFA Franc Zone', in Kirshner (ed.), *Monetary Orders*, p. 80.

13 Emmanuel Farhi, Pierre-Olivier Gourinchas and Hélène Rey, 'Reforming the International Monetary System', Centre for Economic Policy Research, 19 September 2011, p. 21, http://www.cepr.org/content/reforming-international-monetary-system-0.

14 Barry Eichengreen, *Exorbitant Privilege: The Rise and Fall of the Dollar and the Future of the International Monetary System* (New York: Oxford University Press, 2011), p. 130.

15 Ignazio Angeloni et al., 'Global currencies for tomorrow: a European perspective', Bruegel, 23 July 2011, p. 99, http://www.bruegel.org/publications/publication-detail/publication/592-global-currencies-for-tomorrow-a-european-perspective.

16 Carla Norrlof, *America's Global Advantage: US Hegemony and International Cooperation* (Cambridge: Cambridge University Press, 2010), pp. 232–46.

17 Interview with Nicole Gnesotto, Fondation Robert Schuman Newsletter, no. 75, 1 October 2013, http://www.robert-schuman.eu/en/doc/entretiens-d-europe/ee-75-en.pdf.

18 Christian Thimann, 'Global Roles of Currencies', European Central Bank, Working Paper Series, no. 1031, March 2009, p. 21, http://www.ecb.europa.eu/pub/pdf/scpwps/ecbwp1031.pdf.

19 Marsh, 'Australia, Canada dollars classified as reserve currencies', commentary for the Official Monetary and Financial Institutions Forum, 19 November 2012, http://www.omfif.org/intelligence/the-commentary/2012/november/australia-canada-dollars-classified-as-reserve-currencies/.

20 Brendan Kelly, 'China's Challenge to the International Monetary System: Incremental Steps and Long-Term Prospects for Internationalization of the Renminbi', Pacific Forum CSIS, *Issues and Insights*, vol. 9, no. 11, June 2011, p. 13.

21 Monthly Report of the Deutsche Bundesbank, May 1988, p. 22, http://www.bundesbank.de/Redaktion/EN/Downloads/Publications/Monthly_Report/1988/1988_05_monthly_report.pdf?__blob=publicationFile.

22 Jonathan Kirshner, 'Currency and Coercion in the Twenty-First Century', in David M. Andrews (ed.), *International Monetary Power* (Ithaca, NY: Cornell University Press, 2006), pp. 151–53; William W. Grimes, 'Internationalization of the Yen and the New Politics of Monetary Insulation', in Kirshner (ed.), *Monetary Orders*, p. 189.

23 Robin Harding and James Crabtree, 'India takes big step to internationalise the rupee', *Financial Times*, 9 October 2013.

24 Mariya Gordeyeva, 'Kazakhstan pegs tenge to fx basket, dilutes dollar focus', Reuters, 28 August 2013.

25 Speech by Zhou Xiaochuan, 'Reform the International Monetary System', 23 March 2009, http://www.pbc.gov.cn/publish/english/956/2009/20091229104425550619706/20091229104425550619706_.html.

26 Guy de Jonquieres, 'Is Power Really Shifting to China?', *Journal of Economic Diplomacy*, January 2013,

http://eu-asiacentre.eu/pub_details.php?pub_id=84.

27 Lecture by Tommaso Padoa-Schioppa, 'The Ghost of Bancor: the Economic Crisis and Global Monetary Disorder', 25 February 2010, http://www.notre-europe.eu/media/Speech-TPS-LouvainLaNeuve-25.02.2010.pdf.

28 Haihong Gao and Yongding Yu, 'Internationalisation of the renminbi', paper presented to a Bank of Korea–Bank for International Settlements seminar in Seoul, 19–20 March 2009, p.13, http://www.bis.org/repofficepubl/arpresearch200903.05.pdf.

29 Kroeber, 'China's Global Currency: Lever for Financial Reform', Brookings-Tsinghua Center for Public Policy, Monograph Series, no. 3, February 2013, p. 42.

30 Paola Subacchi and Helena Huang, 'The Connecting Dots of China's Renminbi Strategy: London and Hong Kong', Chatham House Briefing Paper, September 2012, http://www.chathamhouse.org/publications/papers/view/185765.

31 Eswar Prasad and Lei Ye, 'The Renminbi's Role in the Global Monetary System', Brookings Institution, February 2012, p. 54, http://www.brookings.edu/~/media/research/files/reports/2012/2/renminbi%20monetary%20system%20prasad/02_renminbi_monetary_system_prasad.pdf.

32 Ibid.

33 Society for Worldwide Interbank Financial Telecommunication (SWIFT), Brussels, Press Release, 8 October 2013, http://www.swift.com/assets/swift_com/documents/products_services/RMB_tracker_September2013.pdf.

34 Prasad and Ye, 'The Renminbi's Role in the Global Monetary System', p. 54; Kelly, 'China's Challenge to the International Monetary System', p. 6.

35 Kroeber, 'China's Global Currency', p. 39.

36 Prasad and Ye, 'The Renminbi's Role in the Global Monetary System', p. 15.

37 Benjamin J. Cohen, 'The Yuan Tomorrow? Evaluating China's Currency Internationalization Strategy', 15 July 2011, p. 9, http://www.polsci.ucsb.edu/faculty/cohen/inpress/pdfs/NPE.pdf.

38 Angeloni et al., 'Global currencies for tomorrow', p. 59.

39 Xiaoli Chen and Yin-Wong Cheung, 'Renminbi Going Global', February 2011, p. 20, http://economics.ucsc.edu/research/downloads/renminbi-going-global.pdf.

40 Kelly, 'China's Challenge to the International Monetary System', p. 22.

41 Edward N. Luttwak, The Rise of China vs. the Logic of Strategy (Cambridge, MA: Harvard University Press, 2012), p. 67.

42 Ibid., p. 244.

43 Yung Chul Park and Chi-Young Song, 'RMB Internationalization: Prospects and Implications for Economic Integration in East Asia', Asia Europe Economic Forum, October 2010, p. 3, http://www.bruegel.org/fileadmin/bruegel_files/Research_contributions/AEEF_contributions/G20_Completing_the_agenda/RoundTable_YC_Park.pdf.

44 Ibid., p. 29.

45 Andrew Higgins, 'Teeing Off at Edge of the Arctic? A Chinese Plan Baffles Iceland', *New York Times*, 23 March 2013.

46 Wendy Dobson and Paul R. Masson, 'Will the Renminbi Become a World Currency?', *China Economic Review*, vol. 20, no. 1, March 2009, pp. 124–35.

47 Kelly, 'China's Challenge to the International Monetary System', p. 23; Cohen, 'The Yuan Tomorrow? Evaluating China's Currency Internationalization Strategy', p. 9; Masahiro Kawai and Shinji Takagi, 'The Renminbi as a Key International Currency? Lessons from the Japanese Experience', paper presented to the Asia Europe Economic Forum, Paris, 10–11 January 2011, p. 6.

48 Eichengreen, 'The Renminbi Challenge', Project Syndicate, 9 October 2012, http://www.project-syndicate.org/commentary/can-china-have-an-international-reserve-currency-by-barry-eichengreen#hhieTSc2jk1PsR35.99.

49 Keiko Yoshioka, 'Yi Gang: Japan, China stand to gain strategic benefits from bilateral currency cooperation', *The Asahi Shimbun*, 21 August 2012.

50 De Jonquieres, 'Is Power Really Shifting to China?', p. 11.

51 Yao Yang, 'America's pivot to Asia will provoke China', *Financial Times*, 12 February 2013.

52 'Defining the Chinese Dream', *Caixin*, 30 January 2013, http://english.caixin.com/2013-01-30/100487911.html?p2.

53 Rudolf Richter, 'European Monetary Union: Initial Situation, Alternatives, Prospects in the Light of Modern Institutional Economics', University of Saarland Economic Series, no. 9908, May 1999, http://www.wiwi.uni-saarland.de/economics-wp/pdf/wp9908.pdf.

CHAPTER THREE

The dollar and US power

By John Williamson

Today the US dollar is undoubtedly the top international currency. This is true for its public and private international roles, whether it is measured as unit of account, medium of exchange or standard of deferred payment – the three traditional roles of money.

The present position of the dollar

Consider first, official use of the dollar. The dollar is the currency most commonly used by countries to express their exchange-rate objectives: at least 37 of the 146[1] currencies of IMF members are pegged to the dollar,[2] while at least 21 claim to float their currency and at least 20 are pegged to some other single currency (mainly the euro) or the Special Drawing Right (SDR).

The US dollar is also dominant in currency intervention (the purchase or sale of a country's currency on the foreign-exchange market to influence its domestic value). Most countries intervene only in dollars. It is the major unit in which

John Williamson was a senior fellow at the Peterson Institute for International Economics from 1981–2012.

official foreign-exchange reserves are held: at the end of the first quarter of 2013, US$3.8 trillion of total reserves amounting to US$11.1tr were in identified dollar holdings, as well as some part of the US$5.1tr in reserves held by central banks unwilling to declare even to the IMF the composition of their holdings.

Similarly, the US dollar dominates private use. It has been estimated in the past that close to half of all international trade was invoiced in dollars,[3] while less than 12% of world trade involved the United States in 2011. Close to 50% of foreign-exchange trading takes place against the dollar.[4] Although the euro had more bond issues than the dollar for a time, most international transactions involve the dollar. And most private international holdings of liquid assets are denominated in terms of dollars (if, unlike equity, they are denominated in anything at all); there are no accurate estimates of the size of these holdings, but they are believed to be much larger than official reserves.

It is thus undeniable that the US dollar presently constitutes the most important component, indeed the vast bulk, of international money. For a time it looked as though the euro might become a serious competitor, but given the recent sovereign-debt and banking crisis in the euro area, it no longer threatens the pre-eminence of the dollar. The Chinese are still taking first steps to establish the renminbi as an international currency, and the use of the yen has shrunk along with the Japanese economy. The same is true of the pound sterling. For the moment, the dollar is unrivalled.

The future of the dollar

Benjamin Cohen lists three factors that determine demand to hold a currency internationally.[5] The first is widespread confidence in the future value of a currency, backed by political stability in the country of origin. Without such confidence, it is impossible to imagine people voluntarily choosing to hold a particular money. The second is what Cohen refers to as 'exchange convenience' and 'capital certainty' – that is, a high degree of transactional liquidity and reasonable stability of asset value. Both of these qualities depend on well-developed financial markets which are open to non-residents. The final factor is a money that provides access to an extensive trans-actional network, which seems to give a strong advantage to larger countries. It is worth noting that his list does not include 'backing' for a currency, which is often held up as a key attribute of an international money. In fact what matters is not an assurance that one will be repaid by an issuer; rather, it is the certainty of being able to find someone else willing to accept the currency. Holders of money do not want the trouble of being repaid.

Consider which currencies are likely in the future to satisfy these conditions. Aside from the renminbi, euro, pound and yen, the Indian rupee may be a possible contender for reserve-currency status at some point. Cohen is right to argue that widespread confidence in the future value of money depends on both political stability and being able to trust the country's authorities not to tolerate inflation. It is in the dimension of political stability that recent travails in the euro area have been particularly damaging, since not all the members of the eurozone (especially Greece and Italy), and certainly their collectivity, can be regarded any longer as politically stable. The secondary reserve currencies – sterling, the yen and the Swiss franc – score relatively well on the political stability crite-rion, but doubts remain about the depth of the UK's attachment to anti-inflationary policy and about Japan's political stability. China is also generally considered politically stable, although there are concerns that, as its population becomes wealthier, it will want a greater stake in how it is governed, and China still has to make the transition to democratic governance (which has often proved stormy). India does not have that particular concern, but faces other challenges. In terms of attachment to price stability, China's record, since hyper-inflation was stabilised in 1951, looks much better than India's, where price stability is seemingly defined as inflation of less than 10%, which is unlikely to impress international investors.

The most widely satisfied criterion is presently the possession of well-developed capital markets that are open to all: not only do the US and the euro area satisfy this condition, but so do all the secondary reserve currencies. Although China and India do not satisfy this condition currently, China has made progress and should be able to fulfil this criterion within 10 or 20 years, so it is likely to prove a temporary block. The same is true of India: if anything, the country seems over-anxious to liberalise its international currency dealings.

But the final factor is the most important to establish a currency's international role. What distinguishes the United States and the euro area from the secondary reserve currencies is the fact that they each have an enormous domestic market. However, if it is accepted that the eurozone is no longer a contender for international status given the political doubts about its future, the key question becomes how long US supremacy will persist. China is already by some measures the largest economy in the world,[6] and will certainly become so within the next few years. Moreover, it is this factor that is likely to propel India's claim to reserve-currency status, since the large size of its population guarantees that it will become the third largest economy in the world unless its growth rate falls far more than is currently anticipated. Alongside an extensive transactional network, which Cohen emphasises, the role of the existing network of users is crucial to internationalise a currency. The fact that the dollar is already used extensively in

London, Frankfurt, Dubai, Singapore, Hong Kong and other international-trade hubs is of vital importance. This factor gives a great deal of inertia to the international role of currencies. Consequently, it appears the dollar will continue to have a great advantage over any other national currency for the next quarter of a century. (However, I would hesitate to forecast for as long as 50 years.)

Rather than an alternative national currency, could the SDR supplant the role of the dollar? Created by the IMF in 1969, the SDR accounts for less than 3% of total reserves and plays no private international role. Barry Eichengreen has argued that it would be necessary to transform the SDR into a private asset if its attractiveness to official holders were to be materially increased, since any use of the SDR as intervention currency would be possible only once the official sector were able to transact with the private sector.[7] This is mistaken, since an important potential role of the SDR is to provide precautionary reserves which do not derive their utility from an expectation that they will be used in intervention.[8] But even on this less demanding criterion, there is no sign of the international community showing such enthusiasm for holding the bulk of their reserves in SDRs, which would be indispensable for an SDR solution to come to pass. Accordingly, an international solution is unlikely. The dollar is likely to remain the top international currency.

The dollar's role and US power

Does the US gain additional leverage by virtue of the international role of the dollar?

The standard economic analysis holds that the United States gains because of the collection of seigniorage. Historically the term seigniorage meant the ability of the sovereign to make a profit when it minted metal into money. In our context the term means the ability to make a profit from international holding of the currency. There are generally considered to be two sources of profit from foreign holdings of the dollar. One arises from holdings of dollar bills by foreigners (in practice, US$100 bills held mainly by drug dealers): in effect, the US gains an interest-free loan when foreigners hold dollar bills. The other arises from the fact that many foreigners wish to hold dollar assets. The preferred form of assets is US Treasury bills, and so the interest rate on them is somewhat lower than it would be otherwise; the savings made are regarded as a part of seigniorage. But the interest saved by the US is merely a few basis points and may be worth even less than the profit yielded by the foreign holdings of dollar bills.[9]

Arguably the real US gain lies in the ability to finance payments deficits without concern and without stockpiling reserves. But the same is true of other developed countries that are able to borrow in their own currencies: the fact that many of them have not run deficits is due to the fact that they have maintained their currencies at reasonable levels, rather than because of an inability to finance a deficit. And insofar as the US is unable to manage its exchange rate as a quid pro quo of the seigniorage benefit, the US loses as a result of the dollar's role.

Economists typically evaluate the reserve role of a currency as a case of trading off the benefits of a country being able to finance payments deficits more cheaply against the costs of losing full freedom to manage its own exchange-rate policy. In the case of the United States, the Dollar Standard involves a bargain whereby the United States gains cheap finance in return for other countries having full freedom to manage their exchange rates. In consequence the exchange rate of the dollar adjusts as a residual. The dollar still acts as the so-called 'nth' currency as it did under the Bretton Woods system, when the

US fixed the dollar price of gold but did not set the exchange rate against other major currencies. In the case of the UK, in the later days of the sterling balances the holders of sterling made it clear that they expected the UK to avoid devaluing in return for continuing to hold sterling. In both cases the advisability of maintaining a reserve role for the currency is determined by one's view of the trade-off between the benefits in terms of financing and the costs in terms of freedom to manage the exchange rate. It is not surprising that many economists have therefore concluded that a reserve-currency role is not advisable.

It has often been argued that the large indebtedness of the United States makes it vulnerable to threats from foreign governments to move holdings out of dollars. But it is a moot point whether the US should fear such a threat. In a world of floating exchange rates, the effect of such a shift would be a dollar depreciation of whatever size was needed to persuade private holders to hold an equivalent volume of dollars. The fact that private holdings of dollars are so much larger than official holdings suggests that this might not be a large depreciation. In any event, there is a countervailing factor: the fear that a shift from dollars of a large foreign holder could reduce its own wealth. As Keynes once observed, when you owe your bank a thousand dollars, you have reason to fear your banker; if you owe it a million, he fears you. In the case of the United States, it owes several trillion dollars to China, and there is nowhere else with financial markets large enough to give China a realistic possibility of moving more than a small fraction of its holdings. Any Chinese threat to move the bulk of these balances would certainly result in dollar depreciation, so the threat would not be credible. Far more credible is the notion that the balances restrain any Chinese inclination to engage in acts that would be regarded as hostile by the United States. This is not to say that China will be submissive to the US in order to defend its dollar holdings; Chinese actors have made perfectly clear that they cannot be blackmailed in this way. Indeed the US values China's continued dollar holdings sufficiently highly to be wary of any language that might suggest it would contemplate actions that could place the dollars in jeopardy. The Chinese leadership is nevertheless bound to be circumspect about threatening to shift out of dollars.

Only China, and possibly Japan, holds dollar balances sufficiently large to face major difficulties in diversifying their holdings. No other countries need to take account of the danger of forfeiting a large part of national wealth should they shift out of the dollar. But this traditional analysis is mainly concerned with the official role of the dollar.

It is difficult to see how US power is enhanced by the widespread private international use of the dollar. For example, the US ability to wage war in Iraq and Afghanistan was in no way dependent upon private international use of the dollar. This seems to be generally true of the use of armed force. Nor is US influence on Pakistan, for example, determined by the dollar holdings of many private foreigners.

There is one large exception: the ability of a country to enforce a financial blockade, such as that currently directed against specified Iranian entities. The United States can order its own companies not to do business with Iran. While this power is present in any sovereign government and is in no way dependent on the role of the dollar, because third countries generally pay Iran in dollars, the US government does have additional leverage. Any payment in dollars ultimately involves a transfer on the books of the Federal Reserve (unless both the recipient and payer of funds have accounts at the same bank, which is unlikely for international payments). The Federal Reserve (Fed) can require that any institution for which it does business has to certify that it either has no prohibited ties to Iran or is in receipt of a waiver. The US can also require that an institution that contracts with the Fed impose similar requirements on the clients on behalf of which it is acting. The Fed does not inspect each transaction, but depends upon financial institutions to do the screening, with stiff penalties possible if prohibited trans-actions slip through. In 2012, when Standard Chartered Bank was accused by the New York State Department of Financial Services of having hidden some US$250 billion of financial transactions with Iran, it had to pay over US$300 million in fines. Thus the US has the ability to stop transactions involving dollars. Insofar as foreign institutions rely on paying with their dollar holdings, and/or Iran relies on receiving dollars, Iran is going to be vulnerable to US economic pressure.

Is there a way to sidestep such pressures? Clearly this is possible by mutual agreement to stop using the dollar. The most likely country to contemplate this is China: instead of paying Iran in dollars, Beijing could pay Iran in renminbi, which could be used by Iran to import from China. Indeed, Iran began to accept renminbi – as well as rupees, yen and South Korean won – for its crude oil in 2012. Even here there is a caveat: the particular Chinese institution that issued the renminbi could be penalised if it was also involved in trade with the United States, since the US government has the power to prohibit US companies doing business with it. Hence China and India began rerouting some renminbi and rupee payments for oil through Russian banks that did not have operations in the US.[10]

While there are few countries the US may wish to block-ade in the same way it has done to Iran, international relations can take unexpected turns. The fact that international finan-cial markets tend to operate in dollars gives the United States a power other countries do not have. It is a power that could be used against any country at a particular point in time. That it is impossible to foresee exactly under what circumstances this power might be used does not mean it should be ignored.

The US dollar is well established in its role as the dominant international money. The one currency that may have contended, the euro, has for political reasons ceased to be a rival. The dollar is unlikely to be seriously challenged in this role in the next quarter century.

The extent to which this gives the US additional power in the world economy is subject to more serious debate. I identify two ways in which the international role of the dollar contributes to US power in the world: by making China more hesitant to jeopardise its relations with Washington; and by strengthening the ability of the US to impose financial blockades on other countries. I have the impression that the additional national power which stems from a dominant international currency tends to be exaggerated by strategic thinkers.

Notes

1 There are 188 members of the IMF, but many of them share currencies, notably the euro, the East Caribbean dollar and the CFA franc. The IMF no longer publishes a table showing the exchange-rate regime of each member, so I examined the country pages in the IMF's International Financial Statistics database. Countries counted as pegging to the dollar were those which showed a constant official rate in terms of the dollar throughout the period; countries with minimal variation; and countries with a constant one-way movement (e.g. consistent with a dollar peg combined with a policy of offsetting inflation by a regular crawl).

2 Richard Dobbs et al., 'An exorbitant privilege? Implications of reserve currencies for competitiveness', Discussion Paper, McKinsey Global Institute, December 2009. MGI has suggested a figure of between 30 and 200 basis points, but even the lower figure strikes me as high.

3 Philipp Hartmann, *Currency Competition and Foreign Exchange Markets: The Dollar, the Yen, and the Euro* (Cambridge: Cambridge University Press, 1998).

4 Bank for International Settlements, Triennial Central Bank Survey: 'Foreign exchange turnover in April 2013: preliminary global results', September 2013, Table 2, p. 10.

5 Benjamin J. Cohen, *The Future of Money* (Princeton, NJ: Princeton University Press, 2004).

6 Arvind Subramanian, *Eclipse: Living in the Shadow of China's Economic Dominance* (Washington DC: Peterson Institute for International Economics, 2011).

7 Barry Eichengreen, 'The Dollar Dilemma: The World's Top Currency Faces Competition', *Foreign Affairs*, vol. 88, no. 5, September/October 2009, pp. 53–68.

8 John Williamson, 'Why SDRs Could Rival the Dollar', Policy Brief, 09-20, Peterson Institute for International Economics, September 2009.

9 Dobbs et al., 'An exorbitant privilege? Implications of reserve currencies for competitiveness', Discussion Paper, McKinsey Global Institute, December 2009.

10 IISS, *Strategic Survey 2012: The Annual Review of World Affairs* (Abingdon: Routledge for the IISS, 2012), p. 66.

CHAPTER FOUR

Financial blockades: reserve currencies as instruments of coercion

By Giri Rajendran

Global powers have a long history of applying economic sanctions to exert geopolitical influence, but a widespread view prevailed until recently that these were relatively ineffective at inducing behavioural change.[1] Indeed, many have argued that previous attempts at imposing trade sanctions have been counterproductive – perpetuating humanitarian suffering while entrenching hardline positions and rallying popular support for errant regimes. In one study, economic sanctions were considered successful in just 34% of 204 cases assessed.[2] Such was the disillusionment with general trade sanctions that by the early 2000s many argued for 'smart sanctions' that more precisely targeted decision-making elites and the entities they controlled.[3]

It is against this backdrop that geopolitical pressure on Iran was markedly ratcheted up in late 2011, principally using economic instruments. The purpose was new: to restrict Iran's hard-currency revenue from oil exports. Three broad sets of measures were used. Firstly, banking sanctions imposed a

---

Giri Rajendran is IISS Research Associate for Defence and Economics.

financial blockade on Iran.[4] Secondly, the European Union instituted an oil embargo. Thirdly, EU sanctions took aim at Iran's ability to ship its exports (particularly oil and petrochemicals) by targeting European-based insurers of oil tankers.

Over the first 18 months the new sanctions increasingly undermined Iranians' confidence in the country's economic prospects and its currency. Between December 2011 and October 2012, Iran's currency, the rial, lost almost 80% of its value against the dollar. Prices for food doubled or even tripled between 2011 and 2012, and overall the IMF estimated that 2012 inflation exceeded 30%, though the exact figure is likely to be higher. Heightened economic uncertainty sharply reduced consumption and business investment, while the sanctions-induced squeeze on government revenue (petroleum exports accounted for some 50% of government revenue in 2012) caused actual revenues to fall short of planned state expenditure by almost 40% in the proposed 2013–14 budget. Official figures show an unemployment rate of 12.5% in urban areas and youth unemployment at 29%, but many believe the latter is closer to 50% (the government counts those who work one hour a week as being employed). As a result, after more than a year's hiatus, Iran was forced to return to the negotiating table without preconditions for talks with major powers, beginning in April 2012, over its nuclear programme. Sanctions also contributed to increased political discontent within Iran, which culminated in the unexpected outright victory of the perceived moderate candidate, Hassan Rouhani, in the June 2013 presidential elections. All this raises the question: what is different about the current sanctions that have made them more effective as an instrument of geo-economic influence?

This chapter argues that it is the use of the dollar that distinguishes the present sanctions regime from previous attempts, which mainly relied on trade restrictions. The differing paths of trade and financial globalisation since the Second World War have steadily diminished the utility of trade sanctions while strengthening the role of the dollar in global banking networks, thereby augmenting the effectiveness of financial curbs. Banking sanctions have also played a pivotal role against Iran, both directly affecting the Iranian economy and reinforcing other areas of the current sanctions architecture. In addition, through their flexible design, banking curbs permit the imposition of follow-on sanctions to thwart Iranian countermeasures. This has injected an unprecedented degree of dynamism into the process, increasing the responsiveness of sanctions to evolving global circumstances and augmenting their overall effectiveness as tools of economic coercion.

Sanctions and the globalisation of trade and financial networks

The globalisation of trade relations following the Second World War was achieved through successive rounds of negotiations undertaken within the framework of the General Agreement on Tariffs and Trade (GATT). Each of these rounds reduced tariffs, quotas and regulatory barriers to foreign goods and services. In the process, global trade networks became highly diversified, particularly during the 1990s after the end of the Cold War. This rapid acceleration in global trade made the implementation of effective unilateral trade sanctions much more problematic. Because of the increasingly dense economic linkages between countries, the imposition of trade sanctions by one state simply resulted in trade diversion to others: as one country severed its links, business opportunities were created for other players, negating the effectiveness of sanctions as an instrument of geopolitical power.

The globalisation of finance since the 1970s followed a different dynamic. In contrast to the diversification of trading patterns, financial networks are largely still centred on or reliant upon the banking systems of advanced Western economies. Indeed, the dollar has played a major role in financial globalisation, a process that has strengthened its role as a reserve currency.

The dollar's ascendancy in global banking became firmly established in the aftermath of the Second World War. There was a huge appetite across Europe for consumer essentials and capital goods for reconstruction. In large measure these were imported from the United States – one of the few Western economies left relatively untouched by the war – and had to be paid for in dollars. However, with Europe having little to export and exchequers across the continent nearly bankrupt from wartime spending, imports were partly financed with dollar loans from the US Treasury Department and US State Department aid, via the Marshall Plan, to allied governments. Thus the dollar became the Western world's reserve currency of necessity, consolidating a position that the US had institutionally entrenched by setting the dollar as the only convertible currency in the Bretton Woods system, the gold-exchange standard which operated from 1944–1971.

Paradoxically, the instability that followed the collapse of Bretton Woods and the subsequent oil shocks further expanded the dollar's global role. In the absence of other viable, liquid currencies to serve as stores of value,[5] the dollar moved from being the advanced world's reserve currency of necessity to the world's reserve currency of choice. Up until the late 1960s, moderate trade and investment flows, alongside the existence of capital controls, meant that cross-border dollar flows occurred mainly via central-banking channels. However, within a decade, the end of the fixed-exchange-rate Bretton Woods system and the removal of many capital controls resulted in a rapid increase in international capital mobility.

The flow of dollars spilled over to the much larger private, commercial and investment banking sectors. As former Federal Reserve Chairman Paul Volcker reflected, 'People were more willing to hold dollars that weren't backed by gold than they were willing to hold dollars that were backed by gold.'[6]

The dollar was so widely accepted that demand for the currency started to expand global banking networks. The euro-dollar markets established in London in the 1960s witnessed a meteoric expansion after the 1973 and 1979 oil shocks as petrodollars were recycled through these lightly regulated banking channels. Offshore financial centres boasting low taxes and/or a high degree of banking secrecy also boomed. The dollar accounted for a significant proportion of the funds flowing through the British Virgin Islands and Bermuda as well as established European tax havens such as Luxembourg and Monaco.

The 'dollarisation' of global banking systems did not stop there. Financial innovation increased the liquidity of the dollar-denominated asset pool. Currency and interest-rate futures were introduced on the Chicago Mercantile Exchange in the early 1970s and rapidly grew to better enable market participants to hedge against (and speculate on) the heightened volatility and economic turbulence of the 1970s and 1980s. In parallel, banks developed a thriving market in over-the-counter exchange-rate and interest-rate swaps. These and other innovations such as credit derivatives (swaps, options and other financial assets that let users manage their risk exposure) further entrenched the central position of the dollar and the US financial system, as a significant proportion of trade in these new instruments involved US-based counterparties and cash settlement in dollars.

Capital-account liberalisation in large parts of the developing world in the late 1980s and early 1990s, and the signing of

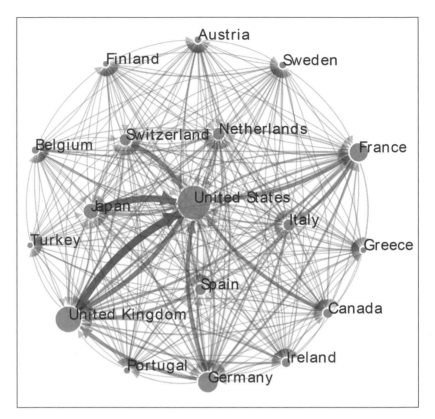

Figure 1. **Bilateral cross-border exposures of major financial centres, 2010**[7]

the General Agreement of Trade in Services (GATS) in 1995, reinforced these trends.

Thus, developments in global banking and financial markets, particularly since the 1970s, have strengthened the international role of the dollar. As the US currency is the main source of global liquidity, the US banking system has come to function as a sort of central processing core through which funds are routed (see Figure 1). Accordingly, it has become correspondingly easier for the US to enforce financial sanctions against peripheral financial centres. The ability of the US, by harnessing large parts of the global banking system, to deploy the dollar as a tool of geo-economic warfare against Iran, is a prime example.

'Weapon-ising' the dollar: the pivotal role of banking sanctions

US banking sanctions were introduced in December 2011, with legislation requiring the president to severely curtail foreign commercial banks' operations of their accounts in the US if they cleared non-petroleum-related transactions with Iran's central bank from March 2012 onwards. A similar ban on oil-related transactions commenced in June 2012. These restrictions would be enforced unless the parent country of the commercial or central bank in question had received an exemption because it was 'significantly reducing' its purchases of Iranian oil. Essentially, this forced foreign banks to choose between access to the US financial system or doing business with Iran. The fact that waivers had to be reissued every 180 days allowed sustained pressure to be brought to bear on Tehran.

The major direct consequence of banking sanctions was that Iran was locked out of leading global payment and credit networks, diminishing its ability to repatriate its hard currency funds held abroad and to engage in foreign trade and investment. Importing country banks refused to process payments for fear of losing access to US financial markets. Even foreign banks without a direct US presence still needed this access to make payments to counterparties via correspondent or 'payable-through' accounts with US banks. By prohibiting US lenders from operating accounts for foreign banks believed to have dealt with sanctioned firms or individuals, US banking sanctions thus constituted a credible threat to most foreign banks. Many also feared the possibility of lawsuits if they inadvertently handled funds later proved to be part of illicit Iranian flows.

Thus, by April 2012, banking sanctions had made it appreciably more difficult for Iran to receive payments for oil exports and were damaging its international trade. While the US granted waivers to countries that demonstrated a commitment to reducing Iranian oil imports,[8] many banks were no longer prepared to take the reputational risk of facilitating Iranian payments and cut links with Iran, despite not being legally required to do so. Even if banks were prepared to risk such transactions, the sanctions made the cost of regulatory compliance prohibitively high. As a result, Iran started accepting payment for its crude in Indian rupees, Chinese renminbi, Japanese yen and Korean won, even though these currencies are not fully convertible. It also encouraged barter – for example, by offering to provide crude in return for wheat, soybean meal, grain and consumer products.

Besides these direct effects, restrictions on banking have fortified three other pillars of the current sanctions architecture: banking sanctions enacted in other jurisdictions, insurance sanctions and oil sanctions.

Part of the effectiveness of US banking sanctions is their impact on transactions in other major jurisdictions such as the euro area. To escape US legislation, as well as to support its own oil embargo on Iran, the EU passed its own banking sanctions.[9] As a result, in March 2012, SWIFT (the Society for Worldwide Interbank Financial Telecommunication), a Belgian firm that provides the secure private network used by almost all banks to send payment messages to one another, took the unprecedented step of expelling Iran's central bank and more than 20 Iranian commercial lenders. Cutting off these banks made it difficult for Iran to complete the large international fund transfers vital to much of its trade.

Banking sanctions also reinforced insurance sanctions due to the close links between the two sectors. Insurance transactions are cleared through banking systems, while insurers often act as partners to commercial and investment banks, providing insurance for payment flows or acting as counterparties to derivatives transactions (contracts that derive their value from underlying assets). Links between banking and insurance are particularly close in some European countries. The threat of US banking sanctions did not drive the EU's decision: the EU implemented its insurance measures several months before the US did. Nevertheless, after the US introduced insurance sanctions, EU insurers – which reinsure 95% of tankers around the world – faced being shut out of US financial markets if they were found to be providing insurance for tanker shipments containing Iranian crude.

Finally, banking sanctions strengthened oil sanctions. While the EU's embargo on Iranian oil imports was significant (the bloc absorbed 20% of Iranian exports in 2011), this measure alone would not have put enough pressure on Tehran. A key factor determining the success of sanctions was whether they forced Iran to reduce its oil exports, rather than simply redirecting shipments elsewhere. According to the US Energy Information Administration, the Asia-Pacific region – particularly China, Japan, South Korea and India – accounted for 60% of Iran's 2.5 million barrels per day in crude exports between January and June 2011. An EU oil embargo, by itself, would have left these exports untouched. More importantly, in the absence of banking sanctions, as EU member states switched to other crude producers, Asian states would likely have taken advantage of the surplus Iranian oil available on the market to increase their imports. Alternatively, third-party states that had not bought Iranian crude previously would have been attracted by the discounts Tehran was offering. In an interlinked world economy, a unilateral EU oil embargo would simply have shaken up global oil-trading patterns. The net effect on Tehran would have been negligible. In order to be truly effective at reducing Tehran's oil exports, sanctions had to be designed to coax cooperation from Iran's non-EU oil-trading partners, many of whom were not nearly as closely allied to the US as EU member states are.

Banking sanctions provided the mechanism to achieve such cooperation. By making exemptions conditional on a country 'significantly reducing' its imports of Iranian oil, and by limiting waivers to six-month periods, the sanctions provided the leverage to apply sustained pressure on all of Iran's import markets. Furthermore, as all new importers of Iranian oil were automatically disqualified from receiving exemptions (and would be subject to banking sanctions were they to begin lifting Iranian crude), third-party states could not offset reduced Iranian exports. For example, Kenya agreed to buy Iranian crude in June 2012, weeks before the EU embargo was due to come into full effect, but subsequently cancelled the contract due to the threat of US sanctions.

As a result, by mid-2013, all of Iran's major trading partners had recorded significant reductions in oil imports compared with 2011 levels. Apart from the EU and South Africa, whose imports fell to zero, large drops were seen in much of Asia: Malaysia (-73%), Sri Lanka (-57%), Taiwan (-57%), Japan (-45%), India (-30%), South Korea (-28%) and Singapore (-25%). Even in China – Iran's largest importing partner and a key ally – a reduction of 21% occurred.[10] Overall, Iran's oil exports halved in 18 months, with further declines likely given that importers must continue paring their purchases to keep qualifying for US waivers from banking sanctions.

Banking sanctions also acted as compliance devices; they were modified to nullify measures taken by Iran and its trading partners to try to circumvent the initial curbs. This flexibility allowed sustained pressure to be brought to bear on Tehran.

For example, banking sanctions were successfully used to counteract a 'gas-for-gold' trade that developed between Iran and Turkey. Although Turkey received a waiver from US banking sanctions for buying less Iranian crude, EU banking sanctions had prevented the repatriation of hard currency to Tehran via the SWIFT network. Unable to transfer funds electronically, Iran had been using Turkish lira payments for its crude, held in Turkish bank accounts, to buy gold, sending the bullion back to Tehran by courier, often via the UAE. As a result, Turkish gold exports to Iran rocketed by a factor of 30 in March 2012 to nine metric tonnes from just 30 kilograms a month earlier. Between March and May 2012, Turkey exported some 58 tonnes of gold to Iran, enabling Tehran to convert US$3 billion of its oil proceeds into gold in spite of sanctions.

In response, Congress passed legislation in August 2012 to levy banking sanctions on entities that permitted funds owed to Iran to be used for anything other than approved purchases such as food and medicine. Even before the law came into effect in February 2013, both Turkey and the UAE had taken measures to curb the 'gas-for-gold' trade. Turkish gold exports to the UAE fell from US$2bn in August 2012 to US$400m in December 2012 as banks and dealers in Dubai suspended trading in Turkish gold bars for fear of being frozen out of global banking systems.

The sanctions net was gradually widened to exert greater pressure on Iran, with the passage of additional legislation in January 2013. The prohibition on operating US bank accounts or correspondent accounts was extended to foreign banks that held, or facilitated dealing in, the Iranian rial; banks that processed 'significant transactions' with Iran's energy, shipping and shipbuilding sectors; and banks that financed business involving Iran's automotive industry. Some of the measures did not even contain exemptions for countries that had scaled back Iranian oil purchases: for example, the provision of underwriting, insurance and reinsurance services or of precious metals, including gold, would trigger automatic sanctions. So would supplying Iran with semi-finished metals and software for industrial functions. The list of activities subject to US sanctions was also lengthened. Firms and individuals (in countries that had not received US waivers) would be black-listed if they provided port-operating services to Iran; bought US banknotes, precious metals, stones or jewels on Tehran's behalf; or supplied goods and services to Iran's automotive sector.

All of these measures, which forced Iran's trading partners to reduce their economic ties, were underpinned by the cred-ible threat of banking sanctions. These were far more effective than other tools of economic coercion available to the US, such as a ban on sanctioned entities bidding for US govern-ment procurement contracts, a ban on US Export-Import Bank credit or guarantees and the denial of US bank loans exceeding US$10m a year.[11] None of these would prevent most foreign firms and individuals from dealing with Iran, given that they were unlikely to be doing business with the US in these areas anyway.

Trade and financial globalisation over the past 70 years have made the dollar an increasingly effective instrument of coer-cion, as evidenced by the current sanctions regime against Iran. Whereas the ability of the US to impose biting trade sanctions has waned, the international role of the dollar, bolstered by the pivotal position of the currency within the global financial architecture, has increased the effectiveness of financial sanc-tions.

Of course, for some targeted states, the perceived costs of compliance – the loss of sovereignty, risks to national secu-rity and the erosion of domestic and regional political power – simply outweigh the economic pain wrought by sanctions, no matter how severe. Nevertheless, the financial blockade against Iran has induced Tehran to cooperate to some degree, so that diplomatic avenues may be explored, while impeding the country's ability to finance its nuclear programme. Tough economic sanctions are one of the few options available to exert pressure on Iran, short of a military strike that could result in a regional war. Ultimately, it is possible that 'in a complex foreign-policy-making environment, economic sanctions may be the least undesirable of a highly undesirable set of alternatives.'[12] Other policy options such as verbal condemnation, rounds of diplomacy and the resort to military force risk being either ineffective or disproportionate. The current sanctions have been more effective than most observers would have predicted when they were enacted and have compelled the regime in Iran to re-evaluate the cost-benefit calculus of its nuclear programme. In the absence of more effective weapons in diplomatic arsenals, the unprecedented use of the dollar to harness the global banking system against Iran may usher in a new era in the use of currencies as instruments of geo-economic power.

Notes

[1] See Brendan Taylor, *Sanctions As Grand Strategy*, Adelphi 411 (Abingdon: Routledge for IISS, 2009), for an overview of these debates.

[2] Gary Clyde Hufbauer et al., *Economic Sanctions Reconsidered*, (Washington DC: United Book Press for Peterson Institute for International Economics, 2007), p. 159. Sanctions were defined a success if they made 'a modest contribution to a goal that was partly realised, often at some political cost to the sender country'.

[3] David Cortright and George A. Lopez (eds), *Smart Sanctions:*

Targeting Economic Statecraft (Lanham, MD: Rowman & Littlefield Publishers, 2002).

[4] US banking sanctions were first instituted by the FY2012 National Defense Authorization Act on 31 December 2011. They were strengthened with the Iran Threat Reduction and Syria Human Rights Act in August 2012. These were subsequently broadened to apply to a wider range of economic activities with the passage of Subtitle D of the FY2013 National Defense Authorization Act, entitled 'The Iran Freedom and Counter-Proliferation Act' in January 2013.

The EU also imposed banking sanctions against Iran in February, March and October 2012.

5   Neither Germany nor Japan was willing to allow their currencies to fulfil reserve-currency functions, largely due to inflationary concerns through an expanded money supply.

6   Craig Karmin, *Biography of the Dollar: How the Mighty Buck Conquered the World and Why It's Under Siege* (New York: Crown Publishing Group, 2008), p. 100.

7   Financial Network Analytics, Tutorial 9, 'Analyzing Cross-Border Banking Exposures', 2010, Quarter 2, http://www.fna.fi/demos/files/tutorial9_full.html?transitionTime =500. The darkness and width of links indicate the degree of bilateral exposure, while the size of the node reflects a country's total exposure.

8   In three rounds of exemptions between March 2012 and June 2013, waivers were granted to several EU member states (Belgium, the Czech Republic, France, Germany, Greece, Italy, the Netherlands, Poland, Spain and the United Kingdom), Japan, India, South Korea, Turkey, South Africa, Malaysia, Taiwan, Sri Lanka, China and Singapore.

9   These were passed through European Council Regulation no. 267/2012 in February 2012 and augmented in March 2012 by European Council Decision 2012/152/CFSP.

10   Kenneth Katzman, 'Iran Sanctions', Congressional Research Service Report RS20871, 26 July 2013, p. 20.

11   *Ibid.*, pp. 8–9.

12   Spyros Economides and Peter Wilson, *The Economic Factor in International Relations: A Brief Introduction* (London: I.B. Tauris & Co., 2001), p. 153.

CHAPTER FIVE

Global trade and global currencies

By Harsha Vardhana Singh

Some macroeconomic realities have changed dramatically in the past 40 years. As an undergraduate student of economics with a focus on development, I learnt the importance of two constraints: the savings constraint and the foreign-exchange constraint. The former refers to the limited pool of domestic savings, which deprives businesses of the credit needed to grow. The latter concerns the difficulty of persuading foreigners to accept the local currency in foreign exchange, thus limiting imports. Of the two, the foreign-exchange constraint seemed more intractable, creating a sense of vulnerability that was always palpable. Ideally, a nation that overcame these two constraints would emerge with a currency that was fully accepted in international transactions and considered a store of value – a reserve currency like the US dollar. But the economic horizon did not show any possibility of a developing country's currency becoming a reserve currency. Today, by contrast, a

Harsha Vardhana Singh is Senior Associate (Strategic Research and Policy Analysis) at the International Centre for Trade and Sustainable Development and Senior Fellow at the International Institute for Sustainable Development. He is a former deputy director-general at the World Trade Organization. The views expressed here are the author's own.

handful of developing economies have the potential to achieve international- or reserve-currency status. Moreover, in the 1970s it was inconceivable that a nation freed of the foreign-exchange constraint could still be subject to a savings constraint; or that the flexibility that a reserve currency provides could allow a country to escape a savings constraint, but in a way that generated huge macroeconomic problems. Yet that is precisely what has happened to the United States.

This chapter sets out the standing of the leading international currencies at present, and assesses the prospects for change in the existing order over the next few decades. With rapid growth in a number of developing countries, powered by trade, the global economic fulcrum is shifting. By dint of their size, the BRIC economies' emergence is having a greater transformational effect than the emergence of the NIC (Newly Industrialised Country) economies had two decades earlier. One indicator of this shift is the increasing use of developing nations' currencies. A multipolar currency world will have an impact on geo-economics and, over time, on geopolitics.

Table 1: **Currency distribution of global foreign-exchange market turnover (percentage shares of average daily turnover in April)**

Currency:	2001	2004	2007	2010	2013
1) US dollar	45	44	42.8	42.5	43.5
2) Euro	19	18.7	18.5	19.6	16.7
3) Japanese yen	11.8	10.4	8.6	9.5	11.5
4) Pound sterling	6.5	8.3	7.5	6.5	5.9
5) Australian dollar	2.2	3	3.3	3.8	4.3
6) Swiss franc	2.3	2.1	2.2	2.7	2.6
7) Canadian dollar	2.3	2.1	2.2	2.7	2.3
8) Mexican peso	0.4	0.6	0.7	0.7	1.3
9) Chinese renminbi	0	0.1	0.3	0.5	1.1
10) New Zealand dollar	0.3	0.6	1	0.8	1

Source: Bank for International Settlements, Triennial Central Bank Survey: 'Foreign exchange turnover in April 2013: preliminary global results', September 2013, Table 2, p.10.
Notes: Percentage shares were calculated for both sides of the transaction. The figures in the table are an average of the two percentages for each country. Adjusted for local and cross-border inter-dealer double-counting (i.e, 'net-net' basis).

International currencies today

As Table 1 shows, the currencies of a few developed econo-mies dominate international transactions. The US dollar, despite a slight decrease, still has a 44% share of daily global foreign-exchange market turnover. The dollar's international dominance is also illustrated by the number of currencies pegged to it. The second-most widely used currency, the euro, has a much smaller share: 17–20%.

Table 2: **Leading exporters and importers in world merchandise trade, 2011 and 2000**

Leading exporters in 2011 (ranked)	Rank in 2000	Leading importers in 2011 (ranked)	Rank in 2000
1) China	7	1) United States	1
2) United States	1	2) China	8
3) Germany	2	3) Germany	2
4) Japan	3	4) Japan	3
5) Netherlands	9	5) France	5
6) France	4	6) United Kingdom	4
7) Republic of Korea	12	7) Netherlands	10
8) Italy	8	8) Italy	7
9) Russian Federation	17	9) Republic of Korea	13
10) Belgium	11	10) Hong Kong, China	9

Source: WTO, International Trade Statistics 2001 and 2012.

Table 3: **Leading exporters and importers in world commercial services, 2011 and 2000**

Leading exporters in 2011 (ranked)	Rank in 2000	Leading importers in 2011 (ranked)	Rank in 2000
1) United States	1	1) United States	1
2) United Kingdom	2	2) Germany	2
3) Germany	4	3) China	10
4) China	12	4) United Kingdom	4
5) France	3	5) Japan	3
6) Japan	5	6) France	5
7) Spain	7	7) India	19
8) India	22	8) Netherlands	7
9) Netherlands	8	9) Ireland	14
10) Singapore	15	10) Italy	6

Source: WTO, International Trade Statistics 2001 and 2012.

Significantly, eight of the top-ten currencies are issued by developed countries, yet five of these do not feature in the top-ten trading nations, as Tables 2 and 3 demonstrate. This result is the same using an alternative measure, namely trade transactions and payments recorded by SWIFT, the Society for Worldwide Interbank Financial Telecommunication.[1] Switzerland, for example, is not a top-ten trading nation but the Swiss franc is the sixth most internationalised currency. The two developing countries with top-ten currencies are China and Mexico. Mexico, despite being part of NAFTA (the North American Free Trade Agreement), a large free-trade area dominated by the dollar, still has a relatively internationalised currency.

Drivers of change in currency usage

A number of factors determine the extent to which a nation's currency is accepted internationally: how much the country is engaged in global and regional trade; the size and structure of the domestic economy; national policies and the quality of institutions; and strategic or political considerations.

1. Global trade

Over the course of the last 20 years, the shares in global trade of Asia, the Middle East, Africa and Latin America have gradually increased, at the expense of those held by the United States and Europe. Tables 4 and 5 chart this shift. The largest increase has been registered by Asia. China and India, in particular, have boosted their global trade over the period.

Trade encourages currency internationalisation over time. At present, for some countries, there is a mismatch between their shares in global trade and the international use of their currencies. However, the present currency rankings largely reflect trade rankings of a few decades ago. Although other factors also affect currency internationalisation, one can

Table 4: **World merchandise exports by region and selected economies, 1993, 2003, 2010, 2011 (billion US dollars and percentage)**

	1993	2003	2010	2011
World (billion US dollars)	3676	7377	14851	17816
Share (percentage):				
World	100	100	100	100
North America	18.0	15.8	13.2	12.8
United States	12.6	9.8	8.6	8.3
Canada	3.9	3.7	2.6	2.5
Mexico	1.4	2.2	2.0	2.0
South and Central America	3.0	3.0	3.9	4.2
Brazil	1.0	1.0	1.4	1.4
Argentina	0.4	0.4	0.5	0.5
Europe	45.4	45.9	37.9	37.1
EU	37.4	42.3	34.7	33.9
Germany	10.3	10.2	8.5	8.3
France	6.0	5.3	3.5	3.3
Italy	4.6	4.1	3.0	2.9
United Kingdom	4.9	4.1	2.7	2.7
Commonwealth of Independent States (CIS)	1.5	2.6	4.0	4.4
Africa	2.5	2.4	3.4	3.3
South Africa	0.7	0.5	0.6	0.5
Middle East	3.5	4.1	6.0	7.0
Asia	26.1	26.2	31.6	31.1
China	2.5	5.9	10.6	10.7
Japan	9.9	6.4	5.2	4.6
India	0.6	0.8	1.5	1.7
Australia and New Zealand	1.4	1.2	1.6	1.7
Six East Asian Traders	9.7	9.6	10.1	9.8

Source: WTO, International Trade Statistics 2011 and 2012.
Notes: These statistics indicate the rough relative importance. For more detail, please see the source. Figures are significantly affected by including the mutual trade flows of the Baltic States and the CIS between 1993 and 2003. Beginning with 1998, figures refer to South Africa only and no longer to the Southern African Customs Union. Figures refer to the EU (12) in 1993, EU (25) in 2003 and EU (27) in 2010. Between 1993 and 2003 export shares were significantly influenced by oil price developments.

generally expect that, eventually, as a country's global trade increases, so will the international use of its currency.

2. Regional trade

For some years now, there have been efforts to better integrate regional markets and even develop regional currency

Table 5: **World merchandise imports by region and selected economies, 1993, 2003, 2010, 2011 (billion US dollars and percentage)**

	1993	2003	2010	2011
World (billion US dollars)	3786	7695	15077	15077
Share (percentage):				
World	100	100	100	100
North America	21.4	22.4	17.8	17.1
United States	15.9	16.9	13.1	12.5
Canada	3.7	3.2	2.7	2.6
Mexico	1.8	2.3	2.1	2.0
South and Central America	3.3	2.5	3.8	4.0
Brazil	0.7	0.7	1.3	1.3
Argentina	0.4	0.2	0.4	0.4
Europe	44.6	45.0	38.9	38.1
EU	35.3	41.3	35.5	34.6
Germany	9.0	7.9	7.1	6.9
France	5.7	5.2	4.0	4.0
United Kingdom	3.9	3.9	3.2	3.5
Italy	5.5	5.2	3.7	3.1
Commonwealth of Independent States (CIS)	1.2	1.7	2.7	3.0
Africa	2.6	2.2	3.1	3.1
South Africa	0.5	0.5	0.6	0.7
Middle East	3.3	2.8	3.7	3.8
Asia	23.7	23.5	29.9	30.9
China	2.7	5.4	9.3	9.7
Japan	6.4	5.0	4.6	4.7
India	0.6	0.9	2.2	2.6
Australia and New Zealand	1.5	1.4	1.5	1.6
Six East Asian Traders	10.3	8.6	9.6	9.5

Source: WTO, International Trade Statistics 2011 and 2012.
Notes: These statistics indicate the rough relative importance. For more detail, please see the source. Figures refer to the Federal Republic of Germany from 1948 through 1983. Figures are significantly affected by including the mutual trade flows of the Baltic States and the CIS between 1993 and 2003. Beginning with 1998, figures refer to South Africa only and no longer to the Southern African Customs Union. Figures refer to the EU(12) in 1993, EU(25) in 2003 and EU(27) in 2010. Between 1993 and 2003 export shares were significantly influenced by oil price developments.

areas.[2] This implies that a significant regional trade presence could increase usage of a nation's currency within that region.

As Table 6 shows, some regions of the world conduct a large part of their total trade internally. For North America,

Table 6: **Intra-regional merchandise trade, 2011 (percentage)**

	North America	South and Central America	Europe	CIS	Africa	Middle East	Asia	World
World	16.4	4.2	38.6	3.0	3.0	3.8	28.8	100
North America	48.3	8.8	16.7	0.7	1.6	2.8	20.9	100
South and Central America	24.2	26.7	18.3	1.1	2.8	2.4	22.5	100
Europe	7.3	1.8	70.6	3.5	3.0	2.9	9.7	100
Commonwealth of Independent States (CIS)	5.5	1.4	51.8	19.5	1.6	3.0	14.8	100
Africa	17.1	3.3	34.5	0.3	13.0	3.6	24.5	100
Middle East	8.6	0.8	12.6	0.5	3.0	8.8	52.8	100
Asia	16.4	3.4	16.7	2.0	2.8	4.4	52.8	100

Source: WTO, International Trade Statistics 2012.

almost half of its total merchandise trade takes place within the region. The equivalent share for Europe is even higher. Africa, on the other hand, conducts far less trade internally than it does with the rest of the world. It is notable that, among emerging regions, Asia stands apart: it conducts over half of its total trade within its own region.

Table 7 shows the regional trade shares of prominent trading nations in 2011. There are several countries that, though not among the top-ten trading nations globally, have a leading role in regional trade. These include Brazil, Canada, Mexico, South Africa and Nigeria. Russia, the ninth largest exporter globally in 2011, also has a dominant role in regional trade. As Table 7 shows, in 2011, its share of regional merchandise trade was 59.8% in imports and 66.1% in exports.

Even if a currency does not have a high international profile, a greater focus on regional trade and currency initiatives – underpinned by trade facilitation and efforts to open markets – will likely lead to regional prominence. Furthermore, the trade shares of these nations are likely to increase significantly over time.

Table 7: **Respective regional merchandise trade shares of selected economies, 2011 (percentage share)**

	Share in regional merchandise trade: imports	share in regional merchandise trade: exports		share in regional merchandise trade: imports	share in regional merchandise trade: exports
USA	73.3	64.9	China	29.2	31.8
Canada	15.0	19.8	Japan	14.3	13.8
Mexico	11.7	15.3	Republic of Korea	8.8	9.3
			Hong Kong, China	8.6	7.6
Brazil	32.3	33.7	India	7.8	5.1
Argentina	10.1	11.1	Singapore	6.1	6.9
			Australia	4.1	4.5
Russian Federation	59.8	66.1	Malaysia	3.1	3.8
			Indonesia	3.0	3.4
South Africa	21.5	16.4			
Nigeria	9.9	19.1			

Source: WTO, International Trade Statistics 2012.

It is notable that the regions with the highest proportion of intra-regional trade (Table 6) also dominate global trade. This suggests that nations with greater intra-regional trade shares, and consequently with currencies widely used within their region, are likely to claim a greater share of global trade and could eventually attain international currencies as well.

3. Supply chains and trade in tasks

In the past two decades there has been a significant increase in the volume of trade conducted through supply chains and trade in tasks.[3] This is because the production process for goods can now be broken down so that different countries produce different components of a product. Apple's iPhone, for instance, while assembled in China, relies on parts and labour from Japan, Germany, South Korea and other countries.[4] Also, with technological changes and growth in foreign investment, there is now major potential for growth in trade in services as part of the supply chain. Such diffusion of tasks implies the need for stable currencies and trade policies. Instability in either case would strain existing linkages through supply chains and discourage new ones. It would hamper the planning of production and inventories as well as accurate estimation of costs. Supply chains would transmit instability beyond a country whose exchange rate was volatile or that introduced arbitrary trade restrictions. In effect, what should be a simple trade decision would turn into a more complex investment decision. Therefore, with the development of trade through supply chains, currencies that are more stable are more likely to internationalise.

Moreover, the expansion of the global middle class that is expected to occur within the next few decades will significantly increase the importance of trade and supply chains to sustain growth and prosperity. This will also generate a substantial increase in foreign direct investment (FDI) and multiple trade and investment links among nations. As a recent study by the World Bank and China's Development Research Center of the State Council put it:

> Continued rapid growth in emerging markets will give rise to an unprecedented expansion of the global middle class (by one estimate, from less than 1.8 billion people in 2009 to about 5 billion in 2030, of whom nearly two-thirds will be in Asia) ... the forces of globalization will remain irresistible, and further cross-border movements of goods, services, finance, people, and knowledge will endure and deepen. Production chains across borders will continue to flourish, and intraindustry and intrafirm trade will intensify.[5]

Thus, we should expect to see the emergence of new countries as suppliers and recipients of FDI. This implies another likely consequence of supply chains: by tying different countries into trade relationships, supply chains will expand the influence of regionalised international currencies.

4. Size and structure of the economy

The gross national income (GNI) of a country also influences the potential internationalisation of its currency. Table 8 lists leading trading nations according to GNI alongside a ranking of their currencies according to international use. The rela-

Table 8: **Gross national income of countries and ranking according to internationalisation of currency, 2013 (billion US dollars)**

	Gross national income	Ranking according to internationalisation of currency
United States	15,735	1
China	7,672	9
Japan	6,106	3
Germany	3,604	2
France	2,743	2
United Kingdom	2,418	4
Brazil	2,311	19
Italy	2,061	2
India	1,890	20
Russian Federation	1,823	12
Canada	1,778	7
Spain	1,391	2
Australia	1,351	5
Mexico	1,160	8
Republic of Korea	1,134	17
Indonesia	844	30
Netherlands	809	2
Turkey	801	16
Switzerland	662	6
Sweden	535	2

Source: World Development Indicators database, World Bank, September 2013; Bank for International Settlements, Triennial Central Bank Survey: 'Foreign exchange turnover in April 2013: preliminary global results', September 2013, Table 2, p.10.
Notes: Figures have been rounded to nearest billion. China includes the figures for Hong Kong.

tively large economies, for example those with GNI over US$1 trillion, bar Brazil, India and South Korea, have currencies that are in relatively wide international use. Moreover, almost all the top-ten trading nations are on the list, even if some rank near the bottom.

The structure of an economy – for instance, its trading profile and the size of its companies – also matters. In international transactions, exporters are eager to limit price fluctuations relative to their competitors and tend to invoice in the currency of their competitors. Importers have a similar objective of avoiding exchange-rate risk and stabilising their costs over time.

Companies conducting large transactions and operating in a large local market are likely to trade in their national currency. Thus, companies with large distribution chains are in a strong position to use their own currency. Similarly, the ability of a country to respond to macroeconomic shocks and to limit instability would encourage international use of its currency.

Exporters in industries facing strong competition or whose goods are close substitutes (except the US) tend not to use their own currency. Likewise, exporters from countries with volatile exchange rates and those forming part of a supply chain would prefer another, more stable currency.

The size, wealth and trading profile of a country will partly determine whether micro-level factors are supportive of currency internationalisation via supply chains. Yet what also matters at the enterprise level are the stability of a currency and the size of the enterprise, transaction or local market – the larger, the better.

5. Macroeconomic and institutional factors
A number of institutional or macro-level factors, if present, help to promote the internationalisation of a currency.[6] Developed financial markets offer liquidity across a wide range of financial

instruments (especially size and depth of the sovereign-bond market). A flexible exchange-rate regime is a hallmark of reserves currencies, guaranteeing that their external value is market-determined. An open capital account ensures that a currency can be easily traded in global markets. Effective and credible fiscal and monetary policies promise low inflation and exchange-rate stability. Credible institutions, such as courts and regulatory agencies, and a well-functioning justice system are important too.

The rising currency powers

It is clear that we are moving towards a multipolar currency world. The trade and economic performance of a number of economies, especially in the developing world, will potentially make their currencies not only regional but also global currencies. An IMF study concluded that the renminbi stands out as the currency with most potential to become widely used internationally.[7] One view holds that the renminbi will be a widely used and traded currency within the next decade; others believe it will take longer. With either timeline, internationalisation will depend on domestic reforms in China.

The renminbi has great international potential due to developments in trade and foreign investment, and a rapid expansion of China's middle class with its associated demands for goods and services. Furthermore, three of the world's 20 commodity-futures exchanges are in China. For these reasons, according to Gregory Chin and Wang Yong, 'increasingly, the consensus Chinese view is that a multi-reserve currency era is coming, even if only gradually, and that it would be in China's strategic interests to promote such a scenario.'[8]

To achieve this, steps are being taken to promote the international use of the renminbi and to limit the potential risks from rapid capital-account liberalisation. The People's Bank of China has signed currency-swap agreements with a score of central banks, totalling RMB2.2tr (US$360bn), to expand the use of China's currency in international trade and financial transactions. A 2009 regional pilot programme to use the renminbi to settle trade in Hong Kong expanded rapidly and is now open to exporters and importers across China conducting trade with any country in the world. By 2012, 12% of China's trade was being settled in its own currency. This has given birth to a dynamic offshore renminbi market in Hong Kong, where the Chinese currency makes up nearly 10% of banking deposits. Banks offer a wide range of renminbi-denominated products and there is an active 'dim sum' market (renminbi-denominated bonds issued outside of China). Despite the renminbi's lack of convertibility, the central banks of approximately ten developing countries – including Malaysia, Nigeria and Chile – are keeping small amounts of the currency as part of their foreign-exchange reserves.

This flurry of activity reflects a three-phase strategy by the Chinese government: to liberalise use of the renminbi for trade and cross-border investment purposes; to open up the capital account in order to provide a much stronger basis for the renminbi; and finally to attain a reserve currency. Reaching this status is likely to be a question of when, not if.

While the renminbi might be the leading candidate to eventually achieve global reserve-currency status, it is important to note that within a shorter timeframe some other currencies could become regionally prominent. These are the currencies of nations with considerable shares of regional trade. The changing patterns of trade, including the increase in supply chains and trade in tasks, suggests that currencies used in regional trade will eventually play a more central role in global trade as well. This trend is even more likely with the expansion of the global middle class and a rise in FDI. These developments will create a more extensive multipolar currency world than is generally anticipated. Thus, many more nations will play a role in shaping geo-economics both regionally and globally. In these circumstances, committed multilateral efforts will be needed to provide greater stability and predictability to the global financial system.

Notes

1   See Figure 1.1 from Marc Auboin, 'Use of Currencies in International Trade: Any Changes in the Picture?', WTO Staff Working Paper, Economics Research and Statistics Division, 1 May 2012, available at http://ssrn.com/abstract=2077974.

2   Rui Cui and Weiyi Wang, 'Regional Currency Cooperation in East Asia: Recent Developments and Prospects', 2012 International Conference on Innovation and Information Management.

3   WTO and IDE-JETRO, 'Trade patterns and global value chains in East Asia: From trade in goods to trade in tasks', 2011, http://www.wto.org/english/res_e/booksp_e/stat_tradepat_globvalchains_e.pdf; 'The Shifting Geography of Global Value Chains: Implications for Developing Countries and Trade Policy', Global Agenda Council on the Global Trade System, World Economic Forum, June 2012.

4   Andrew Batson, 'Not Really "Made in China"', *Wall Street Journal*, 15 December 2010.

5   World Bank and the Development Research Center of the State Council, the People's Republic of China, 'China 2030: Building a Modern, Harmonious and Creative Society', 27 February 2012.

6   'Euro, Dollar, Yuan Uncertainties: Scenarios on the Future of the International Monetary System', World Economic Forum, June 2012,http://www3.weforum.org/docs/WEF_FS_ EuroDollarYuanUncertainties_Report_2012.pdf; Eswar Prasad and Lei Ye, 'Will the Renminbi Rule?', *Finance and Development*, vol. 49, no. 1, March 2012; Peter B. Kenen, 'Currency internationalisation: an overview', BIS Papers, no. 61, January 2012, http://www.bis.org/publ/bppdf/bispap61d.pdf.

7   Samar Maziad et al., 'Internationalization of Emerging Market Currencies: A Balance between Risks and Rewards', IMF Staff Discussion Note, 19 October 2011, SDN/11/17, p. 21.

8   Gregory Chin and Wang Yong, 'Debating the International Currency System: What's in a Speech?', *China Security*, vol. 6, no. 1, 2010, p.144.

CHAPTER SIX

The renminbi's rise and Chinese politics

By Di Dongsheng

Great powers have great currencies and a solid currency helps
to build up power. The People's Republic of China is gradually becoming a great power and the renminbi is an important
part of a grand strategy to accomplish this rise. While various
studies have described the economic effects of China's currency
policy, this chapter explores the non-economic aspects. It seeks
to explain the role that the renminbi has played and is going to
play in China's game plan as well as its political implications,
both domestically and internationally.

China is neither a classic market economy nor a Western-
style democracy. Its policies are not shaped by interest
groups as they sometimes are in the West. On systemically
important matters such as its currency, China's policies are
not a function of short-term, purely economic interests; they
are the result of a series of long-term political and strategic
considerations that aim to protect and expand the power of
the ruling party. The basic logic of the Chinese Communist

Di Dongsheng is an associate professor at the Renmin University of China. The author would
like to acknowledge the extensive assistance of Sabina Asanova, research fellow at Renmin
University of China.

Party's (CCP) justification of its rule to date can be divided into two phases. During Mao's era, the Party declared that 'nobody but the CCP can save China.' Not surprisingly, the leadership adopted an antagonistic posture and even seemed to relish crisis for the first three decades after the republic's founding, coming into conflict with various nations. After 1978, Deng and subsequent leaders based the CCP's legitimacy on the performance of the economy and tried to convince the Chinese people that 'nobody but the CCP can enrich China.' Now we are at a turning point. The new leadership under President Xi Jinping is building its power on new foundations by declaring, 'nobody but the CCP can realise the Chinese Dream.' Precisely what is meant by the Chinese Dream awaits elaboration, but it implies better living standards and greater social security. This points to a major shift in China's economic model away from exports and investment and towards consumption. As such, internationalisation of the renminbi will be an indispensable part of the road map to realise the Chinese Dream. This marks a change from the past 20 years, when the focus was on the renminbi's exchange rate as a strategic tool for China's development and debate centred on whether Beijing was deliberately manipulating the currency to gain a competitive advantage.

The role of the renminbi in China's grand strategy after 1992

Defined by the CCP as a 'Peaceful Rise', China's grand strategy after 1992 was a rather exceptional policy that differed from the generally accepted logic of rising powers. Politically, China took a very low profile in the international arena and seldom vetoed or challenged US policies in the UN Security Council. This behaviour departed from foreign policy during Mao's era, when China was perceived as obstructive and a supporter of pro-revolution movements worldwide.

Economically, China opted to provide various subsidies to foreign direct investors – previously unimaginable for a communist party ever eager to brandish its anti-capitalist credentials. The subsidies for foreign direct investors took the form of tax breaks, cheap land and infrastructure, tax rebates on exported goods, environmental-protection leniency and low wages assured by a trade union that is directly controlled by the CCP. However, the most valuable benefit, not only to foreign investors but to global consumers in general, was the undervalued Chinese yuan.

Between 1994 and July 2005 the renminbi's exchange rate was held stable at RMB8.28 per dollar thanks to dollar purchases in the foreign-exchange market by the People's Bank of China (PBOC), the central bank. The renminbi was then permitted to start rising, but continued intervention by the PBOC kept the pace of appreciation slow so that the exchange rate remained broadly favourable for export industries. Foreign-owned companies account for more than half of Chinese exports. This intervention was tantamount to a tax on the people because the fruits of Chinese labour were not consumed domestically but transformed, via the resulting trade surplus, into increased national savings that were channelled mainly into US Treasury debt. The trade-off was lopsided. The US was in effect borrowing cheaply from China, recycling the money through the US financial system and ploughing it back into China: the stock of foreign direct investment (FDI) in China and earnings retained by foreign investors had reached an estimated 25 trillion yuan by 2013, roughly the same as the country's US$3.66tr in foreign-exchange reserves. Yet, whereas the annual return on FDI in China has been estimated at 15%, China has had to accept low yields on its holdings of US debt. When the effect of dollar depreciation is included, the return has been at best zero. Chinese citizens have been subsidising foreign investors.

Seen in this light, China–US relations over the past two decades can be described as a sort of tributary system, with China constituting one of the main pillars of the United States' well-functioning capitalist system. Many Chinese economists have long been critical of what they see as an irrational deal with the world. But their voices have been ignored by China's decision-makers, who tend to lend greater weight to political and strategic points of view. To strengthen the legitimacy of the ruling party, Chinese leaders believed it was crucial to build a rich, powerful state. Observing the experiences of other East Asian countries, the CCP believed the only way to do this was through industrialisation. Given the poor performance of China's state-owned enterprises since 1949, the leadership looked to international capital for help. The process seemed to be beneficial for both sides and resulted in an odd political marriage between left and right: the world's largest communist party became one of the biggest champions of capitalism overnight. The chief executives of multinational companies and Wall Street money managers suddenly became the most welcomed guests of China's leaders.

Many people were happy with this bargain. The CCP was satisfied because China experienced dramatic industrialisation and rapid GDP growth, which paved the way for the nation's peaceful rise on the world stage. The West was pleased with the 'Great Moderation', a combination of high growth and low inflation that China made possible by subsidising the cost of manufactured goods (at the expense of its own consumers, labour and environment) and exporting savings, which pushed down global interest rates. And the developing world was content because commodity prices boomed due to a rapidly industrialising China's appetite for natural resources.

China's 1.3 billion citizens were less happy with their under-valued currency. Labourers were obliged to work long hours for extremely low wages. Spiralling house prices – inflated, some said, by the domestic currency that the PBOC printed whenever it bought dollars – added to their dissatisfaction. Breakneck industrialisation heightened labour strife, under-lining the lack of rights in China, and caused air and water pollution to reach critical levels.

The deliberate undervaluation of the currency is just one way in which China's economic model diverts financial resources from the people to the ruling party and its affiliated entities. Other channels include financial repression. Because deposit rates are capped, savers receive a meagre interest rate that often does not even keep up with inflation. This enables state-owned banks to funnel cheap loans to state-owned enterprises, whereas small private firms have to pay two or three times as much to borrow money on the black market. Ordinary Chinese also lose out when it comes to 'land finance': local governments buy land cheaply from farmers and urban residents and resell it at high prices to politically well-connected real estate devel-opers, effectively appropriating for the state income that would otherwise have driven private consumption.

These mechanisms all add to the overall financial and fiscal burden that the party-state imposes on society. This 'real tax' level dwarfs the 25% of GDP raised by central and local govern-ments through visible taxes and helps to explain the social unrest that has erupted across China as tension grows between the ruling party and the people. To sum up, China's exten-sive industrialisation has come at the cost of the welfare of the majority of the Chinese people. An undervalued renminbi is one of the root causes of their discontent.

Internationalisation of the renminbi and changing politics

The idea of making the renminbi a global currency was first raised in the late 1990s, when the Chinese authorities realised the high cost of dependence on the US dollar, and gained significant momentum after the 2007–08 global financial crisis. To that end, China has signed more than 20 currency-swap agreements, promoted trade settlement using the renminbi and initiated the development of offshore renminbi centres in Hong Kong, London, Singapore and Taiwan. These arrangements sidestep the need for China and its partners to conduct trade in dollars – a particularly useful advantage at times of international financial stress. Some emerging economies have already included the renminbi in their foreign-exchange reserves.

China is actively debating the appropriate approach to renminbi internationalisation. Some scholars, including Yu Yongding and his colleagues from the Chinese Academy of Social Sciences, are generally wary.[1] They believe that the prevailing policy will encourage disruptive interest-rate and exchange-rate arbitrage between domestic and offshore markets. They also fear that opening up China's capital account will make the economy more volatile. Moreover, laying out a timetable for financial liberalisation will limit the government's room for manoeuvre. These arguments are reasonable but overlook the fact that renminbi internationalisation cannot be viewed exclusively through the lens of economics but must be placed in the wider political and global context.

Some liberal economists advocate renminbi internationalisation as a means of advancing economic and social reforms that stagnated during the decade-long leadership of Hu Jintao.[2] Those reforms include liberalisation of interest rates and the exchange rate, which would fundamentally change the prevailing Chinese economic model.[3] In the 1990s, reformists successfully deployed similar tactics when they used China's WTO accession negotiations as a means of mobilising the whole nation behind painful pro-market reforms. Foreign-policy experts with close ties to the People's Liberation Army also hope to accelerate the pace of renminbi internationalisation. They tend to believe in the great currency–great power nexus, which would require more assertive diplomacy and power-projection capabilities. So far in the debate, it seems that these latter two groups have gained the attention of China's leaders as they chart a road map for reform, suggesting renminbi internationalisation will take centre stage in the coming decade.

Influence on Chinese domestic politics

If the CCP does decide to push forward with renminbi internationalisation, the needed market-orientated reforms will usher in substantial changes in Chinese domestic politics. If reforms lead to a slower pace of foreign-exchange reserve accumulation, China will pay less in seigniorage and more money will be available to be invested and spent at home. If the renminbi begins to be widely used overseas, China will collect seigniorage of its own from foreigners. The development of a broad and deep bond market, necessary if the renminbi is to become a reserve currency, will provide an alternative fund-raising channel for local governments, possibly curtailing the practice of land finance. Premier Li Keqiang has made it clear that he will cut taxes and reduce the size of government. Furthermore, Li plans to reform state-owned enterprises and give market forces greater sway over interest rates and the renminbi's exchange rate.[4] A gradual end to financial repression will erode the profits that state-owned banks and enterprises derive from the private sector.

All these reforms would help to lower the level of real taxation and leave households a larger share of the economic pie. China would be on the road to a consumption-driven economy. Sustaining China's rising living standards is critical to the Party, which is alert to instances of social unrest and growing middle-class dissatisfaction over issues such as pollution and corruption. Under such circumstances, internationalising the renminbi as part of a programme of economic reform would consolidate the CCP's position. Some Western scholars believe that an internationalised currency will even lead to a degree of democratisation in China,[5] though these views are largely wishful thinking. If anything, it is the pressure to democratise that is behind the transformation of China's economic structure and the internationalisation of its currency, not the other way around.

Implications for China's foreign policy

In tandem with a reduction in tension between the Chinese government and its citizens, political strains between Beijing and Washington are likely to mount. China will no longer be willing to play the role of junior partner. China–US ties are likely to become more equal, balanced and competitive – a far cry from today, when, arguably, China in effect pays tribute to the US in the form of a cheap yuan in exchange for stability and prosperity in a US-dominated political and economic system. This embryonic shift was augured in the 'new-style great power relationship' that President Xi proposed to President Obama in 2012. Ironically, US mainstream opinion welcomes the internationalisation of the renminbi in the belief that it will make it harder for China to manipulate what is still seen in the US as an undervalued exchange rate. As such, renminbi internationalisation is perceived as playing to the advantage of the US, which remains preoccupied with its trade deficit. This belief betrays a lack of understanding of other potential consequences once the dollar's exorbitant privilege begins to be eroded.

Just how renminbi internationalisation will affect relations with the US is uncertain. For China's part, the greatest uncertainty has to do with the scope and pace of economic reform. As for the US, swings in the political pendulum will be important. The Democratic Party's labour-union backers and manufacturers will be glad if a rising renminbi restores US competitiveness. By contrast, a diminishing role for the dollar would not go down well with Wall Street or with a Republican administration, especially if a strengthening renminbi makes it harder to curb inflation.

Internationalisation of the renminbi is expected to influence China's foreign policy in other ways. A reformed, rebalanced economy that rapidly increases its imports will give the Chinese government more leverage over other economies, especially as China pays for increasingly more of those imports in yuan. China has repeatedly used economic tools to influence the diplomatic behaviour of other states. Notably, it has managed to limit the global political activities of the Dalai Lama and to deter arms sales to Taiwan. To take another recent example, when a territorial dispute flared up between Beijing and Manila in early 2012, China applied pressure by curbing the import of bananas from the Philippines.[6]

Renminbi internationalisation will also be accompanied by growing Chinese FDI, implying a need for China to protect its overseas assets. To do so, Beijing will have to be capable of projecting power. Time and again in modern history hard power has followed where capital leads, flowing from advanced economies to developing nations regardless of the religion, culture and ideology of the home country. Thus, China is likely to abandon its foreign-policy orthodoxy of non-interference in order to protect its overseas investments.

Against this background, at least three scenarios can be envisaged. The first is a bipolar economic order in which China and the US compete for supremacy and the currency becomes a means to a strategic end. The second – preferred by Beijing – is a multipolar system in which the global economy is much more balanced and no country can run up endless deficits without fear of the consequences. The third is that China fails to build a strong economy and a strong currency and retreats back to being poor and dependent. In this case US hegemony will last for at least another 50 years. All three scenarios are possible. Faced with such uncertainties, China's new leadership is cautious about the potential consequences of renminbi internationalisation. This helps to explain why the CCP's highest officials do not use the phrase in official documents, preferring instead to speak more opaquely of 'cross-border trade settlement in renminbi'.

In the past 20 years, China has abandoned its monetary autonomy and outsourced its currency policy to the US Federal Reserve by pegging the renminbi more or less tightly to the US dollar at an undervalued exchange rate. In doing so, China has ceded the economic well-being of ordinary Chinese and provided extensive subsidies to global consumers and foreign direct investors, notably from the US and its allies. As a result, manufacturing was outsourced to China and helped the country to achieve its dramatic rise. But there has been a price to pay in the form of rising tension between the government and the population as the state imposed a heavy real tax on Chinese society, both explicitly and implicitly.

Successful internationalisation of the renminbi depends on far-reaching reforms, including the gradual opening up of China's capital account and less intervention in setting interest rates and the renminbi's exchange rate. These reforms will entail substantial changes in the Chinese model of development. If implemented successfully, they will reduce domestic political tension as the level of real taxation will fall sharply over time. Despite wishful thinking in the West this will likely help to consolidate the CCP's power rather than usher in democratisation.

In the currency arena, China's traditional dependence on the dollar-based system will gradually give way to more balanced relations as use of the renminbi spreads. Consequently, competition between the great powers will rise and may lead to a bipolar – or tripolar along with the euro area – global political-economic system in coming decades.

Notes

[1] Yin Jianfeng, 'RMB Internationalization: Trade Settlement plus Offshore Market or Capital Account Opening up plus Multinationals? Lessons from Japan's Yen Internationalization', *International Economic Review*, 2011-04, http://en.cnki.com.cn/Article_en/CJFDTOTAL-GJPP201104007.htm; Yu Yongding, 'The Temptation of China's Capital Account', Project Syndicate, 27 March 2013, http://www.project-syndicate.org/commentary/the-risks-of-easing-china-s-capital-controls-by-yu-yongding.

[2] Alistair Thornton, 'Anaemic ascent: Why China's currency is far from going global', Lowy Institute for International Policy, 14 August 2012, http://www.lowyinstitute.org/publications/anaemic-ascent-why-chinas-currency-far-going-global.

[3] Barry Eichengreen, 'The Renminbi Challenge', Project Syndicate, 9 October 2012, http://www.project-syndicate.org/commentary/can-china-have-an-international-reserve-currency-by-barry-eichengreen.

[4] Martin Feldstein, 'China's New Path', Project Syndicate, 29 April 2013, http://www.project-syndicate.org/commentary/the-new-chinese-leadership-s-policy-preferences-by-martin-feldstein.

[5] Eichengreen spells out four challenges for renminbi internationalisation, including the absence of democracy in China. Eichengreen, 'The Renminbi Challenge'.

[6] China buys more than half of the Philippines' exports of bananas, which are the country's second-largest export product.

CHAPTER SEVEN

The new shape of Asia

By Yuriko Koike

The renminbi's role in the global economy must be seen in the context of managing the rise of China within the existing international order, which is perhaps the greatest challenge facing defence and diplomatic strategists today. China is now the world's second largest economy and its biggest holder of foreign-exchange reserves. China's economic strength is allowing it to exert influence in parts of the world where, even a decade ago, its presence was limited. In particular, China has become very active in Africa, where a pattern to its activities has developed: China builds ties with governments irrespective of their human-rights record or whether UN sanctions are in place, with the long-term objective of securing exclusive access to natural resources. Indeed, about one million Chinese are now reported to be living and working across Africa, as part of a new model of mercantilist imperialism China is promoting in the twenty-first century.

China's efforts to secure resources in Africa began in the 1990s but accelerated after Japan ended its official development

Yuriko Koike is a member of the House of Representatives of Japan and former Minister of Defense.

assistance (ODA) to China in 2008 – a decision based on China's rapid economic development and increased defence spending rather than the growing competition for resources. China's incursions into Africa pose challenges for Japan, which, since 1993, has jointly hosted the Tokyo International Conference on African Development (TICAD) every five years. This forum has sought not only to discuss and inform the world of Africa's economic needs but to set agreed standards for investment and trade relations. Meanwhile, China has hosted the Forum on China-Africa Cooperation since 2000. At the July 2012 meeting, former President Hu Jintao announced that China would contribute US$20 billion for Africa's economic development over three years.[1] What is troubling in the announcement is the secrecy of China's African investments. The conference in Beijing emphasised building new strategic partnerships – alliances which the United States and others have begun to see as an alarming form of neocolonialism.

China's exertion of geopolitical and financial influence is not limited to resource-rich developing countries. It had an active approach in Greece even before the country became the epicentre of the European financial crisis. The China Ocean Shipping Company (COSCO) has obtained the right to operate the second pier at Piraeus. A 35-year contract was signed in 2010 for €3.5bn (US$4.7bn), and a truck-loading facility and packaging centre were purchased in the suburbs near Piraeus.[2]

China has also assumed a greater role in Iceland, where the economy particularly suffered during the 2008 financial crisis. In April 2013, Iceland became the first European country to sign a free-trade agreement with China.[3] China has also built a large embassy in the capital, Reykjavik, with an eye to monitoring Arctic shipping and resource developments. According to a 2008 report by the US Geological Survey, 22% of the world's undiscovered accessible oil and natural-gas reserves are located in the

Arctic Sea.[4] China won observer status on the Arctic Council in 2013 and is one of several states actively interested in the northern sea passages, which are becoming seasonally accessible as sea ice melts due to global warming.[5] The first Chinese cargo ship to transit the northeast passage above Russia completed its journey to Europe in September 2013.[6]

The eagle and the dragon

It is in the United States, however, that the power of Chinese money is increasingly felt. China owns at least US$1.3 trillion of US Treasury debt. How might this affect US financial security? The following incident may be helpful to understand the growing concerns in this regard.

In June 1997, Ryutaro Hashimoto, then prime minister of Japan, touched upon the possibility of Japan selling US government bonds during a public appearance in the United States. He said Japan had dreamed of selling large volumes of US Treasury debt on numerous occasions because the US had neglected the obligations of the dollar's reserve-currency role. Holding US government bonds was not the only option available to Japan; another option was to sell the bonds and buy gold, Hashimoto said.

The day after these comments were made, the New York stock market recorded its largest setback in a decade. While an ally such as Japan is unlikely to sell US government securities to an extent that would threaten the US economy, what China will do with its US bonds is less clear. Though it would not wish to see the value of its assets diminish, this concern is unlikely to determine policy in any serious dispute with the US, for example over Taiwan. Indeed, in the future, it is not difficult to imagine that Chinese popular opinion would demand that the country use its financial power if a disagreement over China's so-called 'core interests' escalated dramatically.

For now, China appears to be guarding its foreign-currency reserves judiciously. The make-up of the reserves continues largely to reflect China's trade relations, with the US dollar and euro the principal holdings. Where China's portfolio does not mirror its trade is Japan. So far, Chinese purchases of Japanese government bonds have been negligible, but the potential for China to gain influence over Japan in this regard is real.

China is not the only emerging power with unsettling ambitions. Russia under President Vladimir Putin now appears to be mimicking the United States and executing a Pacific pivot. The aim is to use the country's vast natural resources to gain leverage over Asia's economies and to attract Asian investment to further develop Russia's untapped mineral and energy wealth.

Relations between Russia and Japan are complicated by the fact that the two countries have a long-standing territorial dispute over the Kuril Islands. Bilateral negotiations have made no real progress. While Russia was dealing with its transition from communism, Japan supplied power plants, built houses and has continued to provide medical support for the islands' people. More recently, however, Moscow has displayed greater interest. In 2010, Dmitry Medvedev made the first-ever visit to the islands by a Russian president. Unless the dispute is resolved, Japanese-Russian development projects in Siberia will be impossible. Putin has spent billions on redeveloping the port of Vladivostok, but without the know-how and capital that Japan could bring to Russia, the port might boost China's economy more than Russia's.

China and the IFIs

China's standing within the major international financial institutions (IFIs), principally the IMF, is not commensurate with its economic weight. China is believed to have made a conscious decision not to exert considerable influence over IMF decision-making for now (though it did exact the appointment of a Chinese national – Zhu Min – as a deputy managing director).

However, it might in future wish to expand its influence if it were to further internationalise the renminbi. Following the 2008 financial crisis, China's contribution to the IMF was set to increase to 6.4% of the organisation's funding, third behind the 17.7% contribution of the United States and 6.6% from Japan. In 2012, at a G20 summit in Mexico, the BRICS also pledged to contribute more in the midst of the European debt crisis; their total funding commitment exceeded US$70bn.[7] In return, emerging-market states were seeking greater voting shares and representation in the IMF – reforms agreed upon in 2010.

If quota reforms were carried out, China would become the third largest voting shareholder in the IMF (India, Brazil and Russia would also join the top ten). However, the US has yet to ratify the agreement, which has been held up in Congress for some time.

While the changes in voting shares are held up, the next stage of reforms cannot go through. In this context, China is looking at alternatives to existing arrangements; specifically, the BRICS bank. This new development bank seeks to help finance development projects in the BRICS countries and prevent a future financial crisis by, for example, pooling foreign currencies. Despite high hopes that the BRICS bank could help lay the foundation for a new global financial architecture, it has made little progress so far – largely due to difficulties agreeing on details between member countries.

Overall, challenges remain for China if it seeks to accommodate the internationalisation of its currency with a greater role in IFIs. It is unclear how exactly China hopes to use the renminbi's rise as a geopolitical tool. The country's opacity calls for caution.

Notes

[1] Ben Blanchard, 'China strengthens Africa ties with $20 billion in loans', Reuters, 19 July 2012.

[2] Yuriko Koike, 'The great global bargain hunt', Live Mint, 1 July 2012.

[3] Andrew Trotman, 'Iceland first European country to sign free trade agreement with China', The Telegraph, 15 April 2013.

[4] US Geological Survey Newsroom, '90 Billion Barrels of Oil and 1,670 Trillion Cubic Feet of Natural Gas Assessed in the Arctic', 23 July 2008, http://www.usgs.gov/ newsroom/article.asp?ID=1980#. UnDx43DIbFA.

[5] Shiloh Rainwater, 'Race to the North: China's Arctic Strategy and Its Implications', US Naval War College Review, vol. 66, no. 2, Spring 2013, pp. 62–82.

[6] Tom Mitchell and Richard Milne, 'First Chinese cargo ship nears end of Northeast Passage transit', Financial Times, 6 September 2013.

[7] Raymond Colitt, 'BRICS to Announce IMF Contribution at G-20 Meeting, Brazil Says', Bloomberg, 18 June 2012.

CHAPTER EIGHT

The international monetary system: past, present … and a possible future?

By Robert B. Zoellick

The power of currencies – their purchasing power and wider influence – is exercised through the international monetary system of the era. In considering the roles and weight of reserve currencies, and the challenges posed by possible aspirants, it is useful to place today's international monetary issues in historical perspective: in effect, we are struggling with some 'unfinished business' of the Bretton Woods design.

Benn Steil's recent book, *The Battle of Bretton Woods*, sets the stage.[1] As Steil explains, Harry Dexter White, the US policy architect at the Bretton Woods conference of 1944, wanted a new international monetary system to end competitive currency devaluations and trade protectionism – the twin scourges of the 1930s, from the US perspective.

Reflecting the times, the New Deal Treasury also wanted to: eliminate the old European powers as rivals on the world

Robert B. Zoellick is a Distinguished Visiting Fellow at the Peterson Institute for International Economics and Senior Fellow at the Belfer Center for Science and International Affairs at Harvard University's Kennedy School of Government. He is former president of the World Bank.

stage, in part by breaking Britain's imperial trade preference; elevate the US dollar to the status of surrogate gold; and shift the focus of power for the United States' monetary system from Wall Street and the Federal Reserve Bank of New York to Washington and the Treasury Department.

John Maynard Keynes, White's British counterpart, wanted a new monetary system that would support liberalised trade while keeping global payment imbalances from emerging – and if they did emerge, allow them to be corrected with minimal economic pain.

The core difference in perspective reflected differing national circumstances. The United States, a country with massive reserves and a big trade surplus, was not concerned with global imbalances in 1944. Britain, deeply in debt, with few reserves and uncertain export prospects, wanted the new monetary system to create a type of international central bank to encourage the growth of money globally, with mechanisms to press surplus countries to increase imports or appreciate their currencies.

Keynes and Britain lost that argument. (Ironically, 66 years later, US Secretary of the Treasury Tim Geithner tried to revive Keynes's logic with a proposal to establish a norm for current-account surpluses in the G20.)

There are, nevertheless, four legacies of that 'Battle of Bretton Woods' that we should recognise in considering today's debates.

Firstly, both White and Keynes treated the problem of reviving multilateral trade – and eliminating discrimination and trade-depressing barter arrangements – as a currency problem, not a trade problem. Yet over the years, their successors let global currency and trade issues become detached, managed in different global institutions, the IMF and WTO, without acting on the policy linkages.

Secondly, the international monetary and trade systems are still struggling with the 'rebalancing' issue: how to share the adjustment between surplus and creditor countries.

Thirdly, White's victory – the enthronement of the US dollar – survived long after his international monetary system collapsed. This result is ironic, given that White did not believe the dollar could play an ongoing global role without the firm backing of gold.

The benefits of the US dollar's rank as the principal reserve currency have been frequently commented upon, especially by those who are envious. The US government can issue debt and print money freely. It gains from seigniorage, as people hold dollars for use in transactions. As the world has seen, especially in recent years, control of dollar-clearing systems enables the United States to limit others' financial access. Many global goods, especially commodities, are priced in dollars. These benefits also provide the United States with political gains and soft power.

As Fred Bergsten of the Peterson Institute for International Economics has pointed out, however, this international role for the US dollar comes with two big costs: firstly, other countries can determine their exchange rate with the dollar – and avoid appreciation – by buying dollars; and secondly, a moral hazard that the United States will not be pressed to adjust its domestic policies as its imbalances rise.[2]

Bergsten and his colleague Joe Gagnon have pointed to sizeable trade costs for the United States, with a considerable impact on jobs.[3] Gagnon has identified more than 20 countries that have been intervening directly in foreign-exchange markets to influence their currency values, so as to strengthen their economies and create jobs at home. The result has been a build-up of reserves exceeding US$10 trillion. Bergsten estimates that the United States is the largest absolute loser from these intervention policies, which have expanded US trade and current-account deficits by US$200–500 billion per year. These figures amount to at least half of all US external imbalances, and Bergsten suggests these added imbalances have cost the United States 1–5 million jobs when unemployment is already high.

Bergsten explains that the problem of 'currency manipulation' is not just an issue for the United States. The euro area is the second-largest loser, with serious effects on some southern European crisis countries.

The fourth legacy of the White–Keynes debate is intellectual caution among policymakers. Steil describes how Keynes came to age intellectually during the First World War, when much that was taken for granted in terms of the world's political and economic foundations came crashing down: 'In particular, the gold standard – and with it, indelibly fixed exchange rates – seemed as natural to people then as it seems strange to them now.'

Steil explains that the issue of replacing the gold standard with something else was as fraught with difficulty as the issue of replacing the dollar globally today. The 'extreme' of purely floating exchange rates was considered by few economists in the 1930s – Lionel Robbins being a notable exception – to even be 'a system' that could help restore equilibrium.

Today's floating-rate system and heavy reliance on central banks and their monetary policies may also not be immutable. In 1937, Freidrich von Hayek argued that floating rates would eventually lead to disastrously destabilising capital flows. Milton Friedman, who was more sanguine about floating exchange rates, nevertheless blamed central banks' misguided money supply policies for the stagflation of the 1970s.

Germany and France never abandoned their determination to fix exchange rates in Europe. They created the euro in 1999, although the euro area, like the global system, still faces issues of adjustment between surplus and deficit countries.

In 2009, Governor Zhou Xiaochuan of the People's Bank of China observed that 'the frequency and increasing intensity of financial crises following the collapse of the Bretton Woods system suggest that the costs of such a [floating] system to the world may have exceeded its benefits.'[4]

In sum, we are indeed still discussing the 'unfinished work' of Bretton Woods. And changes in the global economy will likely require us to reconsider old intellectual strictures. Indeed, I suspect that the combination of structural shifts in the global economy and extraordinary monetary policies will push the topic of the future international monetary system higher up the agenda.

Over the past five years, about two-thirds of global growth came from developing countries. As recently as the 1990s, their percentage contribution was below one quarter. Over the past decade, exports from developed to developing economies increased from 25% to 45% of developed countries' exports.

In the 1990s, developed countries held almost 70% of the world's reserves; today, the developing countries hold 70%. Of course, developing economies will face their own challenges of continued growth and productivity. The eventual withdrawal of today's extraordinary monetary policies, best exemplified by quantitative easing, will influence their asset values.

Yet the structural point will remain that the norms the G7 countries had developed to manage a world of floating exchange rates after the breakdown of the first Bretton Woods system in the early 1970s may not be accepted by other principal states in the new global economy.

This structural shift has come at the same time that economies, especially developed ones, have been struggling to recover from the Great Recession. An unprecedented crisis evoked an extraordinary response from central banks: monetary policy has been used to buy time and limit tail risks. As a result, monetary policies are in uncharted territory.

Exceptional monetary policies, adopted primarily for domestic policy reasons, conducted wholly in domestic currency, differ from intervention policies affecting the exchange rate. But the lines may blur. The anxiety about competitive currency devaluations, for example, has increased trade frictions.

If monetary policies lead to asset price bubbles that plant the seeds of more shocks, the managers of the international monetary system will have to cope with additional stress.

The members of the WTO and IMF have actually agreed to articles that offer multilateral standards for addressing the manipulation of exchange rates that lead to unfair trade problems. Article XV of the General Agreement on Tariffs and Trade states that economies shall not use exchange rate actions to 'frustrate' the agreements to open trade, although the WTO is to defer to the IMF in making assessments. Article IV of the IMF requires economies to 'avoid manipulating exchange rates or the international monetary system to prevent effective balance of payments adjustment or to gain an unfair competitive advantage...'[5]

Yet these articles have remained dormant. At a minimum, the members of the IMF and the WTO need to discuss what they mean by these terms – to which they have, after all, agreed. The head of the IMF, in particular, but together with the director general of the WTO, should not abdicate the responsibility to address these issues, because they are fundamental to the 'unfinished business' of managing imbalances. Inattention could lead to dangers to the trading system and could frustrate a sustainable global economic recovery. These questions are at the heart of the future international monetary system.

The leaders of the international system need to anticipate possible problems raised by structural shifts in the global economy; responses to the Great Recession; extraordinary monetary policies with uncertain implications; and a rising debate about competitive devaluations. If multilateralism fails, unilateralism may prevail.

Of course, in considering 'new business', we start from the system we have inherited. I believe the US dollar will remain the principal reserve currency for years to come. The dollar has held steady at 60% of global reserves over the past decade, after declining from 70%. With the euro area's troubles, the euro's share has slipped; developing economies now hold about 24% of their reserves in euros, down from 31% in 2009. Other currencies – Swiss, Australian, Canadian – increased their attractiveness for a time, but their market size is limited and cyclical conditions have dampened some interest. The Japanese yen and British pound will play a modest role. SDRs, which represent less than 3% of global reserves, suffer from a lack of private trading, invoicing, borrowing and lending.

Over time, if China opens its capital account, as its leaders have continued to pledge to do, I expect the renminbi will play a greater role in the international monetary system. Yet managers of reserve assets look for a combination of credit, liquidity and returns. For some years to come, the renminbi's use will be handicapped by strict exchange controls and capital markets that are underdeveloped and state-directed.

As China's role in the international monetary system increases, the United States and the European Union, home to today's two principal reserve currencies, will have to address long-term fiscal challenges and a departure from extraordinary, experimental monetary policies.

At some point, the challenge for the international order will be to manage a multiple reserve currency system that is stable and can contribute to larger goals of growth with low inflation, open trade and efficient movements of capital.

Such a system could add discipline to domestic fiscal and monetary policies. The discipline would not be as strict as under the old gold or gold-exchange standards but it could limit the moral hazard that has led some to criticise the US dollar and its privileges.

In order to work, however, a competitive, multi-reserve currency monetary system – in effect, a new international monetary system – needs to be grounded in norms and practices that are generally understood and accepted.

I would not expect such a new monetary system to be agreed through a grand treaty or global convocation. Near the end of his book, Steil provides a useful reminder that no one actually created the classical gold standard system. That system emerged through trial and error over centuries without any formal agreement. Therefore, those who speculate about future monetary arrangements should keep in mind the possibility of 'accumulating incrementalism', rather than a grand design.

The 'power of currencies' is best expressed – like the power of militaries – by deterring wars and achieving a peaceful stability that enables individuals and countries to pursue opportunity and prosperity. One 'currency of power' can achieve such stability but with costs to its ability to adjust. Multiple 'currencies of powers' may also be able to provide a stable and prosperous system – if they operate within an understood international monetary regime. That is the future challenge for the major economic powers.

Notes

1   Benn Steil, *The Battle of Bretton Woods: John Maynard Keynes, Harry Dexter White, and the Making of a New World Order* (Princeton, NJ: Princeton University Press, 2013).

2   C. Fred Bergsten, 'Currency Wars, the Economy of the United States and Reform of the International Monetary System', Stavros Niarchos Foundation Lecture, Peterson Institute for International Economics, Washington DC, 16 May 2013, available at http://www.piie.com/publications/papers/bergsten201305.pdf.

3   Joseph E. Gagnon, 'The Elephant Hiding in the Room: Currency Intervention and Trade Imbalances', Working Paper Series, 13-2, Peterson Institute for International Economics, March 2013.

4   Speech by Zhou Xiaochuan, 'Reform the international monetary system', 23 March 2009, http://www.bis.org/review/r090402c.pdf.

5   Principles and Procedures of IMF Surveillance, http://www.imf.org/external/pubs/ft/history/2012/pdf/4a.pdf.

CONCLUSION

By Alan Wheatley

'Currency power figurations are never static. They evolve along predictable lines with the growth and decline of nations.'

Robert Mundell

Currencies have been in the arsenal of state power for centuries. Some of the first coins made in China 2,500 years ago were in the shape of a knife. A trusted currency enables a government to raise resources in a crisis, either with cash – as US secret agents did to buy the loyalty of warlords in Afghanistan – or on credit. The United States, boasting the most powerful armed forces and the only dominant reserve currency, has easily financed deficits, via the bond markets, that would have forced other countries to cut spending at home and perhaps scale back their ambitions abroad. Washington has had to do neither.

Power and influence

The US has deployed the power of the dollar in changing ways over the years. In the 1970s and 1980s the purpose was

Alan Wheatley is Global Economics Correspondent at Reuters.

frequently to shift the burden of balance-of-payments adjustments on to others – or at least to share it more equally. At times the US went down the route of quiet dollar diplomacy; other times it was brutally direct in its willingness to talk down the dollar in order to get even friendly governments to implement economic policies that favoured the US.

In recent years, the US has had less success on this front. One reason is that Germany, which runs a big current-account surplus, is part of a currency bloc whose overall external-payments position was broadly in balance until the financial crisis struck. The other reason is that China, now the biggest surplus nation, has largely ignored US demands. When Beijing has consented occasionally to let the renminbi rise ahead of key US bilateral meetings, it has usually managed to extract policy concessions in return. At the margin, the distribution of power has shifted.

In the diplomatic sphere, the United States has used the dollar as a coercive instrument mainly to press Iran to negotiate over its nuclear programme. In an earlier century, the dominant power would have enforced its economic and political interests by dispatching the navy. Today, computers that route instantaneous money transfers serve the same purposes as gunboats once did. The US can exercise leverage because of the central role the dollar plays in world commerce and investment, thus enabling Washington to largely exclude Tehran from the global payments system. The dollar's pivotal role – mirrored and reinforced by the global dominance of US banks – also feeds into disproportionate US influence over regulatory trends and the management of international crises.[1]

Jonathan Kirshner has drawn the distinction between such deliberate attempts at policy influence, which he terms 'enforcement', and the indirect exercise of monetary power, or 'entrapment', which occurs when the foreign users of a dominant currency fall into line passively. The latter description broadly fits the countries of the Gulf Cooperation Council (GCC), which, with the exception of Kuwait, have preserved their pegs to the dollar even when the US currency's weakness in 2007 and 2008 pushed up their inflation rates to uncomfortably high levels. It is certainly a description that fits China, which has generated dangerous economic imbalances as well as US$3.66 trillion in reserves as a result of tightly managing the renminbi's exchange rate against the dollar. Because China cannot easily unload its reserves, John Williamson in Chapter Three identifies Beijing's ensuing policy entrapment as one of only two ways in which the international role of the dollar contributes to US power in the world. The second is US control of dollar-clearing networks, which allows for targeted sanctions of the kind directed against Iran.

There are broader views of dollar power. The US reaps billions of dollars in seigniorage – interest-free loans – when foreigners choose to hold dollar bills. Like the government, US corporations can borrow conveniently in their own currency at interest rates that are much lower than they otherwise would be if the dollar were not in strong demand by central banks and money managers. Most commodities, notably oil, are denominated in dollars, as are their corresponding futures contracts. And the dollar is used more widely than any other foreign currency in hotels and bazaars across the globe. Indeed, it is no exaggeration to say that the world operates on a dollar standard. A sharp rise in yields on US dollar bonds in the summer of 2013, after the Federal Reserve (Fed) served notice that it would start withdrawing the extraordinary monetary stimulus it was providing the US economy, was quickly transmitted around the world. Capital flooded out of emerging markets to capture higher returns in the US, prompting emergency policy responses from India to Indonesia and Turkey.

Challenging the dollar's dominance

It is this power and influence wielded by the US – a legacy of the central role reserved for the dollar under the Bretton Woods regime – that a growing number of countries want to check. Europe has done so to some extent by creating the euro, which, though still a work in progress, has shielded its members from the worst of the monetary turbulence exported by the US. For its part, China realises that if it wants to help write the rules of an evolving multipolar currency system it must first promote the renminbi beyond its borders.

Unfortunately for those who would like to weaken the dollar's standing – and China is not alone – history shows that inertia favours the incumbent. Contributors to this volume outline how a new multi-faceted currency order is emerging. Nevertheless, the consensus is that the dollar will remain at the apex of the currency pyramid for the foreseeable future, given the economic power that the US derives from its unrivalled leadership in technology and finance as well as in defence.

Still, enough holders of dollar reserves are sufficiently worried that US fiscal profligacy will eventually undermine the currency that they are hedging their bets by shifting gradually into other currencies. As Robert Zoellick says in Chapter Eight, the world is still dealing with the 'unfinished business' of Bretton Woods. An international monetary order that relied less on the dollar would, in principle, be good for global financial stability. The current system does not exercise discipline on surplus countries such as China to adjust – something the far-sighted John Maynard Keynes wanted to build into the Bretton Woods system, only to be overruled by the US, then a surplus country itself. Nor does it incorporate adjustment incentives for the US, now in perpetual deficit, because of the reserve role of the dollar.[2] Yet by running trade deficits in order to supply all the safe-haven dollars that reserve managers want to own, the United States is undermining the very fundamentals that make the dollar attractive in the first place – the so-called Triffin Dilemma.[3]

The world attempted to create an alternative reserve currency to the dollar in the late 1960s with the Special Drawing Right (SDR), but, to the regret of John Williamson, it never became a privately held asset. Governments settle their business with the IMF in SDRs, so issuing one of the currencies that comprise the SDR basket – currently the dollar, euro, yen and sterling – confers prestige and possibly influence. That is why China would like the renminbi to be included. But Zhou Xiaochuan's dream of the SDR developing into a global reserve currency is likely to remain just that. It is hard to disagree with Barry Eichengreen: 'No global government, which means no global central bank, means no global currency. Full stop.'[4]

Instead, the dollar is likely to cede ground over time, if for no other reason than US share in the global economy – a critical criterion for a reserve currency – will keep shrinking as emerging markets catch up. Sensing this, central-bank reserve managers are making diversification from the dollar a priority. In one informal survey by an investment bank, only about one-quarter of reserve managers expected the dollar to be the top reserve currency in 20 years. The presumed alternative was not another currency, but a portfolio of currencies.[5] Harsha Vardhana Singh presents the case, in Chapter Five, why more currencies are likely to acquire a regional, or even global, role as a result of shifting trade patterns.

But, as Zoellick argues, a new order is unlikely to come about through a 'grand treaty or global convocation'. Unless confidence in US fiscal and monetary policy evaporates, there is little prospect of a headlong flight out of the dollar, not least because of doubts over the prospects for its two most widely touted rivals, the euro and the renminbi, which is explored in

Chapter Two. As a result, while global economic power will become more evenly distributed among the US, the euro area and China over the next decade or two, the process will be piecemeal.

It will be impossible for the euro and the renminbi to challenge the dollar's supremacy without far-reaching political changes to permit the partial mutualisation of debt in the euro area and financial-market liberalisation in China. It would be rash to rule out either in the long run. The eurozone was close to collapse before ECB chief Mario Draghi's dramatic intervention in July 2012 demonstrated yet again the resolve of Europe's elite to make a success of the euro. The outlines of a more stable institutional framework for the single currency are slowly taking shape.

China's currency strategy?

In China, it is hard to identify many power brokers who would benefit from scrapping the current model of crony communism. Allowing private actors, not the party-state, to allocate savings and investment would erode the basis of Communist economic and political power. As 2013 wore on, China's state media was abuzz with speculation that far-reaching financial-liberalisation measures were in the pipeline. But policy changes to date have been incremental. Only the People's Bank of China, which executes policy but does not formulate it, has a clear interest in wholesale reform. Moreover, China's leaders are not obviously ready for the global responsibilities that reserve-currency status entails; they are preoccupied by domestic issues, well aware that social and political stability at home is vital for the regime's survival. [6]

But it pays to keep an open mind. Circumstances can change. In the late 1990s it was still assumed that the Japanese yen would be Asia's principal currency. The renminbi was barely mentioned in the literature of the time. Economic necessity might force the hand of the Communist Party and create the springboard for China's currency eventually to grow into something greater than a 'junior yen'.[7] In any event, the future of the renminbi as at least a secondary reserve currency seems assured. Di Dongsheng explains in Chapter Six how internationalisation of the renminbi is central to the Communist Party's economic- and political-reform strategy. The practice of paying for exports and imports in renminbi can only expand in tandem with the Chinese economy, which is poised to overtake the United States' before long to become the largest in the world. Chinese tourists and businessmen will appreciate the convenience of being able to use their home currency more readily overseas, and they will do so with pride. The renminbi will also benefit from reserve diversification: Asian countries with ever closer economic ties to China have practical reasons for holding the currency; those farther afield can do no harm to their relations with China if they pay tribute to the country's global renaissance by buying some of its bonds. Several states, mainly in emerging markets, are already doing so. That is startling progress for a country where foreigners had to use foreign-exchange certificates, instead of banknotes, up until 20 years ago.

Still, serious questions remain about China's capacity to turn the growing international use of the renminbi into strategic power. This book has shown, in Chapter Two, that a country with monetary influence wields such power. Sometimes that requires coercion. At other times, soft power will suffice: countries with close economic and political ties to a dominant state have a natural interest in the stability and reach of that state's currency. This is one of the paths China is pursuing. Yet Beijing, despite ever stronger trading relationships, is making uneven progress in winning hearts and minds. It has antagonised neighbours in Asia with its uncompromising territorial claims, as Yuriko Koike spells out in Chapter Seven, while in Africa its aggressive investment has triggered charges of neocolonialism. Opacity and intransigence, the hallmarks of a repressive single-party state, also hinder China's ability to exert the soft power that extends a currency's reach (and vice versa). Perhaps it is an accident of history that the issuers of the present and previous reserve currencies were democracies. But perhaps it is not.

Towards a multi-currency system

Overall, Williamson's conclusion is judicious: because of inertia, the dollar will retain a great advantage over any other national currency for the next quarter of a century, but forecasting 50 years ahead calls for caution.

What would be the geo-economic implications if a multipolar reserve-currency system were indeed to emerge? In the best of all worlds, coordination among a G3, made up of the US, the euro area and a renminbi-led bloc in Asia, would reduce global imbalances and associated volatility in exchange rates and capital flows. The currency wars decried by Brazil and others – when the US prioritised reviving its domestic economy post-crisis rather than worrying about foreign-exchange spillovers – would give way to a revival of attempts made in the 1980s to keep exchange rates within broadly agreed bands, perhaps monitored by the IMF on pain of sanctions.

The US does not want to surrender currency power. But if the renminbi became more attractive to international investors due to market-orientated reforms in China, Washington would surely regard that as a triumph for its economic diplomacy. The US has been the loudest advocate for the domestic financial reforms China needs to pursue, followed by the phasing out of capital controls, to enhance the renminbi's international appeal. As long as the US maintains strong economic fundamentals, the consequences of a reduced role for the dollar need not be a significant threat to the United States' economic well-being. Indeed, the emergence of plausible alternatives to the dollar could serve as a positive source of discipline on US economic decisions.[8]

Some think this is naïve. The US cannot be expected to accommodate China's monetary rise any more readily than it will accept China's military rise. In the words of Jonathan Kirshner:

> States do and will continue to seek to extend the international use of their currency in order to increase their political influence ... As long as there are states and money, states will attempt to manipulate monetary relations to advance their political objectives.[9]

Following this line of thought, currency rivalry could grow more, not less, intense. An expanding euro area will be in a stronger position to resist US demands and press for policy concessions of its own should the US need help one day. As for China, it is fettered by its vast pile of dollar reserves. China cannot dump those dollars without doing itself untold harm. But the US cannot erect trade barriers against China or other big foreign creditors – to show its disapproval of their perpetual surpluses – without triggering protectionism and a financial-market panic. This is the financial equivalent of mutually assured destruction. As Joseph Gagnon puts it, China resents the dollar's privileged position while the US chafes at the persistent current-account deficits forced on it by massive reserve accumulation. Tensions could ensue that a more symmetric system – one perceived as fairer – would help to ease.[10]

Fairness is certainly central to Chinese thinking. As PBOC Vice-Governor Yi puts it:

> We think the global financial system dominated by the dollar will remain unchanged for some considerable length of time. If, however, China, Japan, European nations and emerging countries increase the use of their own currencies in trade and investment, that would help create a new, fairer international financial order.[11]

Some of the ways in which China's currency power might shape that order are already becoming apparent. Latin America has been in the US sphere of influence since the Monroe Doctrine was set out in 1823. But with increasing Chinese investment in Latin America's natural-resource sectors, Beijing's political clout in the region can only grow. China's state-owned policy banks have made big loans to several Latin American countries; the PBOC has opened renminbi credit lines with Argentina and Brazil; and Chile has invested some of its currency reserves in the renminbi. It is plausible to imagine that in a future balance-of-payments crisis Latin America could turn to China – or a Chinese-led BRICS bank – for a bailout rather than to the IMF, which is widely seen as a US proxy. Beijing would perhaps be able to attach conditions to any aid that might, for example, give it preferential access to resources or port facilities. Washington would surely regard such developments in its backyard as provocative.

Another potential flashpoint is the global payments system. In Chapter Four Giri Rajendran illustrates how the US has imposed biting sanctions against Iran by preventing the Islamic Republic from clearing dollar payments through the Federal Reserve. This is an extremely effective form of currency power that Beijing might be able to exercise itself once China's own international renminbi-clearing system is operational and the renminbi is more widely used for trade. Keeping the Chinese system open to an ally that is under Western sanctions would, at the very least, invite tensions and misunderstandings.

China's ravenous appetite for raw materials could also provide the impetus for some countries to start pricing commodities in renminbi, eroding one of the pillars of the dollar's strength. China is the leading consumer of most major metals, including copper, nickel and aluminium, and of many agricultural commodities. Its import volumes are likely to keep rising even as the pattern of its economic growth shifts. Brendan Kelly argues that 'this rationale could prove particularly compelling for use of the yuan [RMB] by resource-dependent economies in Africa, for example, with large percentages of their national incomes derived from commodities exports.'[12]

In the same vein, Gulf energy producers will have an incentive in coming decades to carry out a pivot of their own towards Asia, away from the US and Europe. For the boom in shale gas and oil is steadily reducing US energy imports, while fast-growing Asia's thirst for energy seems unquenchable. Indeed, China overtook the United States as the world's leading oil importer in 2013. A study by the IMF in 2012 noted the increasing importance of developing Asia's growth cycle for the Saudi economy.[13] As more oil pipelines, tankers and gas terminals are built to transport Gulf oil and gas to Asia, with manufactured goods increasingly flowing in the other direction, the two regions are already forging closer political and financial ties. It might therefore be logical for the Gulf, at some point, to diversify its reserves away from the dollar and towards the renminbi.

Syed Abul Basher, a researcher with the Qatar Central Bank, believes all members of the GCC should abandon their long-standing peg to the dollar and establish their own currency so they can set monetary policy independently of the US. This was the reason why Kuwait broke ranks with the GCC and abandoned its dollar peg in 2007: the Fed's policy was too inflationary for an economy booming from sky-high oil prices. If the GCC's oil and gas exports were priced in the new currency, a sizeable market for it would immediately emerge and the new currency could mature into a major international money in the long run, Basher argues.[14]

True, the Gulf states rely on the US for their defence and would not drop the dollar lightly. But Australia is also a military ally of the US, and that has not stopped the country from shifting 5% of its reserves into renminbi to reflect its burgeoning trade and investment links with China. The sum is modest but it is an indication of the international role that Canberra expects the renminbi to play.

In a generation's time, a US that might be close to self-sufficiency in energy would still have a strategic interest in guarding the world's sea lanes and chokepoints so that oil and gas keep flowing. Arguably, for the US to remain a leading power in Asia, it must guard the oil supply from the Gulf to the Pacific. But so would China. And by then the *Liaoning* will no doubt be one of only several Chinese aircraft carriers capable of carrying out such a mission. Also, at that point, there is every chance that a rapidly ageing China will be running a current-account deficit and will need to attract foreign capital to fill the gap. A strong convertible reserve currency buttressed by benignly deployed military muscle would help it do just that.

These scenarios are necessarily speculative because the Communist Party has not set out its long-term thinking. But it would be natural for a country of China's size and with China's interests to covet both military and currency power. The two go hand in hand. And long-term planning is one of the Party's strengths. As one political science scholar in China put it:

> I would think that our leadership does have a strategic purpose behind the internationalisation of the

RMB. That no public statement or research has been identified could be a sign that they prefer to keep it low-profile. After all, the Americans will be hyper-sensitive about a strong alternative currency.[15]

How China fleshes out that strategic purpose, and how the US and others respond, are among the questions that will define this Asian century.

Notes

1   Eric Helleiner, 'Below the State: Micro-Level Monetary Power', in David M. Andrews (ed.), *International Monetary Power* (Ithaca, NY: Cornell University Press, 2006), p. 79.

2   Ignazio Angeloni et al., 'Global currencies for tomorrow: a European perspective', Bruegel, 23 July 2011, p. 35, http://www.bruegel.org/publications/publication-detail/publication/592-global-currencies-for-tomorrow-a-european-perspective.

3   Paul Volcker and Toyoo Gyohten, *Changing Fortunes: The World's Money and the Threat to American Leadership* (New York: Random House, 1992), p. 39.

4   Barry Eichengreen, *Exorbitant Privilege: The Rise and Fall of the Dollar* (New York: Oxford University Press, 2011), p. 141.

5   Stephane Deo and Ramin Nakisa, 'Where is consensus?', UBS Investment Research, 19 December 2012.

6   David Daokui Li, 'Is China Ready for Global Economic Leadership?', China Changing Lecture 2012, Lowy Institute for International Policy, Sydney, 19 April 2012, http://www.lowyinstitute.org/events/china-changing-lecture-2012-china-ready-global-economic-leadership-professor-david-daokui-li.

7   Arthur Kroeber, 'RMB Rising: Lessons from History', *China Economic Quarterly*, March 2012, p. 39.

8   Linda Goldberg, 'The International Role of the Dollar: Does It Matter if This Changes?', Federal Reserve Bank of New York Staff Report, no. 522, October 2011, p. 3, http://www.newyorkfed.org/research/staff_reports/sr522.pdf.

9   Jonathan Kirshner, 'Currency and Coercion in the Twenty-First Century', in Andrews (ed.), *International Monetary Power*, pp. 155, 161.

10 Joseph Gagnon, 'Toward a More Symmetric International Currency System', China Finance 40 Forum, 24 April 2012, http://www.cf40.org.cn/plus/view.php?aid=5247.

11 Keiko Yoshioka, 'Yi Gang: Japan, China stand to gain strategic benefits from bilateral currency cooperation', *The Asahi Shimbun*, 21 August 2012.

[12] Brendan Kelly, 'China's Challenge to the International Monetary System: Incremental Steps and Long-Term Prospects for Internationalization of the Renminbi', Pacific Forum CSIS, *Issues and Insights*, vol. 9, no. 11, June 2011, p. 15.

[13] Niklas Johan Westelius, 'External Linkages and Policy Constraints in Saudi Arabia', International Monetary Fund Working Paper, no. 13/59, 5 March 2013.

[14] Syed Abdul Basher, 'Regional Initiative in the Gulf: Search for a GCC Currency', paper presented to the IISS Geo-economics and Strategic Conference 'Currencies of Power and the Power of Currencies', Bahrain, 30 September 2012, http://www.iiss.org/en/events/geo-economics%20seminars/geo-economics%20semi-nars/archive/currencies-of-power-and-the-power-of-currencies-38db/syed-abul-basher-98f4.

[15] Private communication.